CASE STUDIES ON SEXUAL ORIENTATION AND GENDER EXPRESSION IN SOCIAL WORK PRACTICE

CASE STUDIES ON SEXUAL ORIENTATION AND GENDER EXPRESSION

IN SOCIAL WORK PRACTICE

EDITED BY **Lori Messinger and Deana F. Morrow**

COLUMBIA UNIVERSITY PRESS   NEW YORK

COLUMBIA UNIVERSITY PRESS
Publishers Since 1893
New York Chichester, West Sussex

Library of Congress Cataloging-in-Publication Data
Case studies on sexual orientation and gender expression in social work practice / edited by Lori Messinger and
Deana F. Morrow.
    p. cm.
   Includes bibliographical references and index.
   ISBN 0–231–12742–1 (alk. paper) — ISBN 0–231–12743–X (alk. paper)
   1. Social work with gays—Case studies. 2. Sexual minorities—Counseling of—Case stuides. I. Messinger, Lori.
II. Morrow, Deana F.
   HV1449.C36 2006
   362.8—dc22   2005038046

∞

Columbia University Press books are printed on permanent and durable acid-free paper.

Printed in the United States of America
c 10 9 8 7 6 5 4 3 2 1
p 10 9 8 7 6 5 4 3 2 1

To Frances E. Tack, MS, LPC, LCAS, NCC
Boo Tyson, MDiv, and
The members of Educators and Friends of Lesbians and Gays (EFLAG)

CONTENTS

PART 5 **POLICY AND RESEARCH** 103

CONTRIBUTORS

LORI MESSINGER, PHD, MA, MSW, is an assistant professor and the director of the BSW program at the University of Kansas School of Social Welfare in Lawrence. She received her doctorate in social work, as well as her master of social work degree, from the University of North Carolina at Chapel Hill and also holds a master of arts in political science from Rutgers University. An award-winning instructor, Dr. Messinger teaches courses in social welfare policy, political advocacy, multicultural social work, qualitative research, human sexuality, and program planning. Her practice background is in the fields of sexual assault and domestic violence services, public health education, and social program planning. Dr. Messinger's primary areas of research include comprehensive community planning processes, cultural competence in social work education, feminist theories and research methodologies, and lesbian and gay studies. She holds memberships in the Council on Social Work Education and the Social Work Baccalaureate Program Directors Association, where she is a founding member of Educators and Friends of Lesbians and Gays. She has served as a board member for Equality Alabama, an organization working to advance full equality and civil rights for all the people of Alabama through education and action.

DEANA F. MORROW, PHD, LPC, LCSW, ACSW, is an associate professor of social work at Winthrop University in Rose Hill, South Carolina. She received her doctorate in counselor education from North Carolina State University, a master of social work degree and a graduate-level certificate of gerontology from the University of Georgia, and a master's degree in counseling from Western Carolina University. Dr. Morrow teaches micro and mezzo practice courses at both the graduate and the undergraduate levels. Her practice background is in clinical practice in the fields of mental health, aging, and health care, and her research focus is in the areas of social work practice with sexual minority populations and social work education. She is a licensed professional counselor and a licensed clinical social worker in the state of North Carolina, and a member of the Academy of Certified Social Workers at the national level. She holds memberships in the National Association of Social Workers and the Council on Social Work Education, where she has a national appointment to the Council on Sexual Orientation and Gender Expression. She is also a certified site visitor for the reaccreditation of social work education programs through the Council on Social Work Education.

CAROLYN A. BRADLEY, PHD, MSW, LCSW, CADC, is a student assistance counselor in a New Jersey public school.

HARRIET L. COHEN, PHD, LMSW-ACP, is an assistant professor in the Department of Social Work at Texas Christian University, in Fort Worth.

ELIZABETH CRAMER, PHD, is an associate professor in the School of Social Work at Virginia Commonwealth University, in Richmond.

EILEEN DEHOPE, PHD, BCD, LCSW, is an associate professor in the undergraduate Social Work Department at West Chester University, in West Chester, Pennsylvania.

SANDRA DONNELLY, PHD, is a lecturer in the social work program at the University of Houston at Clear Lake.

STEPHEN ERICH, PHD, is the BSW director and an assistant professor in the social work program at the University of Houston at Clear Lake.

MARCIE FISHER-BORNE, MSW, MPH, is a doctoral student in the School of Social Work at the University of North Carolina at Chapel Hill.

ELISE M. FULLMER, PHD, is an associate professor and the BSW program director in the Department of Social Work, Criminal Justice, and Gerontology at Murray State University, in Murray, Kentucky.

PATRICIA L. GREER will complete the master of social work degree in 2005 at the University of North Carolina at Charlotte. She earned her bachelor of social work degree in August 2003, magna cum laude, at UNC-Charlotte, with minors in religious studies and sociology.

KRISTINA HASH, MSW, PHD, is an assistant professor in the Division of Social Work at West Virginia University, in Morgantown, where she received her MSW and her graduate certificate in gerontology.

PATRICIA M. HAYES, MDIV, MSW, is a social worker in Syracuse, New York.

DAVID HENTON, BA, MSSW, is the assistant field director at Texas State University at San Marcos.

NANCY A. HUMPHREYS, PHD, is a professor of policy practice and the director of the Institute for the Advancement of Political Social Work Practice at the University of Connecticut School of Social Work, in West Hartford.

DAVID JENKINS, PHD, is an associate professor and the associate director of the Department of Social Work at Texas Christian University, in Fort Worth.

ROBERT H. KEEFE, PHD, ACSW, is an associate professor in the School of Social Work at the State University of New York, Buffalo.

ARLENE ISTAR LEV, CSW-R, CASAC, is a social worker, family therapist, and educator addressing the unique therapeutic needs of lesbian, gay, bisexual, and transgender people. She is the founder of Choices Counseling and Consulting (info@choicesconsulting.com; www.choicesconsulting.com) in Albany, New York, providing family therapy for GLBT people. She is also on the adjunct faculties of the State University of New York, Albany, School of Social Welfare, and Vermont College of the Union Institute and University.

DONNA MCINTOSH, MSW, is an associate professor and department chair of the Social Work Department at Siena College, in Loudonville, New York.

CHERYL A. PARKS, PHD, ACSW, is an associate professor at the University of Connecticut School of Social Work, in West Hartford.

CATHRYNE L. SCHMITZ, PHD, is a professor and the director of the School of Social Work at Radford University, in Radford, Virginia.

GLENDA F. LESTER SHORT, PHD, LCSW, is an assistant professor and the MSW program director at Southwest Missouri State University–Springfield/Joplin.

SELLO SITHOLE, MSW, DPHIL, is a senior lecturer in social work and social science research at the University of Limpopo in South Africa.

JOSEPHINE TITTSWORTH is a student in the social work program at the University of Houston at Clear Lake.

JANET WRIGHT, PHD, is an associate professor at the University of Wisconsin at Whitewater.

D. R. YONKIN, CSW, is a psychotherapist at Harris Rothenberg International, an employee assistance program in New York City.

Lori Messinger

SOCIAL WORK educators often draw on their own experiences in teaching, using illustrations from practice experiences and personal lives to help students better understand the concepts and skills taught. Yet instructors' experiences are necessarily limited; they cannot claim to have experience with every population, situation, and issue. Further, it is important to recognize that students get a perspective that is shaped by their professors' own class, gender, culture, race, ethnicity, age, ability, and sexual identity, as well as the identities of those with whom the educators have contact. This limitation can cause a bias in social work education toward those dominant identities that describe the majority of educators: middle-class, middle-aged, white, female, able-bodied, typically gendered, and heterosexual.

Most educators recognize these limitations and use a range of techniques to expose students (and themselves) to additional perspectives, including fiction and nonfiction readings, films, immersion activities, and guest speakers. Another method used by social work educators is the case study. Case studies have been part of social work education for many years. A cursory review of published collections of case studies reveals casebooks on direct practice (Haulotte & Kretzschmar, 2001), group work (Shulman, 1968; Shulman, Lotan, & Whitcomb, 1998), spiritual issues in practice (Scales et al., 2002), administration and management (Schatz, 1970; Young, 1985), macro practice (Fauri, Wernet, & Netting, 2004), and social work with the aging (Wasser, 1966).

Case studies in social work education are designed to "elicit discussion and analysis of situations and to build the students' capacity to clearly define issues, problem-solve, make appropriate…decisions, [and] implement, and evaluate selected solutions" (Jones, 2003, p. 84). These case studies have several elements in common: they are based on actual practice-related situations; they provoke questions that do not have a clear answer but instead invite thoughtful debate and discussion; they are short enough to read in class; and they tell stories in a way that engages the student reader both intellectually and emotionally. Good cases challenge students to consider how they would apply the theories and research findings that they learn in class to a complex situation that might occur in their practice. This casebook was developed with these guidelines in mind. The cases included herein present a variety of client systems, issues, concerns, strengths, supports, and intervention methods in a way that is designed to elicit student reflection and enhance student learning.

This casebook is a companion to our textbook, Sexual Orientation and Gender Expression in Social Work Practice (Morrow & Messinger, 2005). Both books address a need in social work education to meaningfully include information about affirmative practice with gay, lesbian, bisexual, and transgender client systems. While the textbook could be used in a class focused exclusively on practice with GLBT populations, we have designed the individual chapters so that they could be incorporated into social work courses that are required for the BSW and MSW degrees, as well as into many elective courses. The casebook adopts a similar strategy, with cases that could be used in a variety of social work courses. Each case study is accompanied by a list of corresponding chapters in our textbook, along with additional readings, to assist students in acquiring an understanding of the theoretical concepts and empirical research findings that inform each scenario.

The casebook is loosely divided into five parts: (1) individuals, (2) couples and families, (3) groups, (4) organizations and communities, and (5) policy and research. Within each part, cases address diverse issues—such as coming out, spirituality, addiction, disability, workplace issues, poverty, HIV infection, and homophobia—and specific populations—including GLBT elders, youth, and people of color. A chapter index grid (see table 1) helps instructors to identify the cases that are most appropriate to their topic areas.

Instructors typically use cases as the basis for in-class discussions, exercises, role-playing, and other reflective and interactive activities. To this end, each case study is followed by a set of questions that instructors can use to stimulate class discussion. The authors also have included an experiential activity for use with each case, along with the purpose, structure, instructions for implementation, suggested courses for use, and the time and materials necessary.

REFERENCES

Fauri, D. P., Wernet, S. T., & Netting, F. E. (Eds.). (2004). Cases in macro social work practice (2nd ed.). Boston: Pearson Education.

Haulotte, S. M., & Kretzschmar, J. A. (Eds). (2001). Case scenarios for teaching and learning social work practice. Washington, DC: Council on Social Work Education.

Jones, K. A. (2003). Making the case for the case method in graduate social work education. Journal of Teaching in Social Work, 23(1/2), 183–200.

Morrow, D. F., & Messinger, L. (2005). Sexual orientation and gender expression in social work practice: Working with gay, lesbian, bisexual, and transgender people. New York: Columbia University Press.

Scales, T. L., Wolfer, T. A., Sherwood, D. A., Garland, D. R., Hugen, B., & Pittman, S. W. (Eds). (2002). Spirituality and religion in social work practice: Decision cases with teaching notes. Washington, DC: Council on Social Work Education.

Schatz, H. A. (Ed.). (1970). A casebook in social work administration. New York: Council on Social Work Education.

Shulman, J. H., Lotan, R. A., & Whitcomb, J. A. (1998). Facilitator's guide to groupwork in diverse classrooms: A casebook for educators. New York: Teachers College Press.

Shulman, L. (1968). A casebook of social work with groups: The mediating model. New York: Council on Social Work Education.

Wasser, E. (Ed.). (1966). Casebook on work with the aging: Ten cases from the Family Service Association of America project on aging. New York: Family Service Association of America.

Young, D. R. (Ed.). (1985). Casebook of management for nonprofit organizations: Entrepreneurship and organizational change in the human services. New York: Haworth.

TABLE 1 Chapter Index

CHAPTER	TITLE	AUTHOR	LESBIAN	GAY	BISEXUAL	TG	ELDERS	YOUTH	PEOPLE OF COLOR	COMING OUT	SPIRITUALITY	ADDICTION	DISABILITY	DEATH AND DYING	WORKPLACE	POVERTY	HIV	HOMOPHOBIA
1	Passages: From Feeling Woman to Being Woman	Stephen Erich, Sandra Donnelly, & Josephine Tittsworth				X				X					X			
2	Finding Hope: The Case of Randall	Patricia L. Greer & Deana F. Morrow		X					X									
3	The Covert Life of Philip Johnson	David Henton			X		X		X		X				X			
4	Brian at the Crossroads: A Case Study	Sello Sithole			X				X	X					X			
5	Young, Transgender, and Out in East Los Angeles	David Henton				X		X	X						X			
6	The Military Life: The Case of Saundra	Patricia Greer & Deana F. Morrow	X						X	X					X			
7	Shonda Harrison: A Young Transgender Client in Jail	Patricia M. Hayes & Robert H. Keefe				X		X	X								X	
8	Sandy Miller's Competency, Religious Beliefs, and Homophobia	Glenda F. Lester Short	X						X	X						X		
9	Ronald Jackson: A Man on the "Down Low"	Robert H. Keefe & Patricia M. Hayes		X	X				X									
10	Thelma Without Louise: The Story of an Aging Woman Who Identifies with Women	Elise M. Fullmer	X				X					X						
11	Are We a Family Now? The Case of Morgan, Shea, and Alex	Cheryl A. Parks & Nancy A. Humphreys	X															
12	The Case of Joan and Terri: Implications of Society's Treatment of Sexual Orientation for Lesbians and Gays with Disabilities	Eileen DeHope	X															
13	A Family in Transition	Cathryne L. Schmitz & Janet Wright	X						X									
14	From Lesbian Relationship to Trans/Lesbian Relationship	Arlene Istar Lev	X			X			X	X								
15	Alan's Story: A Heterosexually Married Couple Faces a Sexual Identity Crisis	David Jenkins		X						X								
16	Seeking a Child Through International Adoption: Lucy's and Robin's Story	Nancy A. Humphreys & Cheryl A. Parks	X															
17	Making Difficult Decisions	Harriet L. Cohen	X				X				X			X				
18	Jack and Karen: A Transgender Love Story	Carolyn A. Bradley				X					X	X	X					
19	Who's Your Daddy?	Lori Messinger		X					X									
20	The Day We Shared Our Coming Out Stories	Elizabeth Cramer	X		X				X	X					X			

TABLE 1 (continued)

CHAPTER	TITLE	AUTHOR	LESBIAN	GAY	BISEXUAL	TG	ELDERS	YOUTH	PEOPLE OF COLOR	COMING OUT	SPIRITUALITY	ADDICTION	DISABILITY	DEATH AND DYING	WORKPLACE	POVERTY	HIV	HOMOPHOBIA
21	Homeless Because I Am Different! Homeless Youth: Stories from the Field	Donna McIntosh		X		X		X	X	X								X
22	Gender Identity Case Histories	D. R. Yonkin				X		X		X								X
23	"Building Excuses" in the Workplace	Kristina M. Hash	X						X									X
24	Designing a Strategy for Changing Agency Policy	Nancy A. Humphreys & Cheryl A. Parks	X	X											X			
25	Making the Link: Domestic Violence in the GLBT Community	Marcie Fisher-Borne	X	X	X													
26	A Leap of Faith: Southern Ministers Organizing for Change	Marcie Fisher-Borne																X
27	Hate Crime Laws: Making a Difference	Lori Messinger	X	X									X					X
28	A Policy Analysis of a Constitutional Amendment: Implications for Aging Populations	Lori Messinger	X	X	X		X											X
29	Getting It Right: Doing Research with GLBT Youths	Lori Messinger	X	X	X	X		X	X	X								X

PART ONE

INDIVIDUALS

THE CASES in this section focus on gay, lesbian, bisexual, and transgender people. Some stories are told in the first person, others are told as more traditional "case histories." Although the cases describe individuals, each case has implications for the larger systems of which each person is a part: families, workplaces, human service agencies, communities, and policy arenas. Instructors can use these cases with students to help them see the connections between the individuals who come into their offices and the many systems that shape their worlds.

In chapter 1, a transgender BSW student recounts her personal identity and surgical transition from male to female. Readers should consider both the psychological issues described and how her transition will affect her experiences in her social work program. Chapter 2 presents a clinical case study of a young African American gay man who has survived a difficult childhood. Chapter 3 presents another African American man, one who is older and married to a woman but struggling with his sexual desires for men. The men in both cases are affected by dynamics in their familial systems and in larger institutions, including the child welfare system and the military. The conflicted interactions between the clients and their social systems can spark important class discussions.

The story of a South African man in crisis is told in chapter 4, which describes his meetings with his employer's employee assistance program. Students can use this case to compare and contrast cultural, social, and political structures in South Africa and the United States. Juanita, the transgender Latina described in chapter 5, negotiates financial, familial, and medical concerns, while Saundra describes one soldier's experience with the "don't ask, don't tell" policy of the U.S. military in chapter 6. Shonda Harrison, the transgender client in chapter 7, calls a social worker from the local prison; students can use her story to examine the clinical, familial, and institutional issues presented in this case. Using these chapters, students can plan interventions on individual, organizational, community, and policy levels.

Instructors can use the last three cases in this section to challenge students to understand the cultural, social, religious, and economic forces that sustain prejudice and oppression of GLBT people. The focus of chapter 8 is not the client but the social worker, who has to confront her own biases and fears in order to work with a client who discloses same-sex erotic feelings. Ronald, the client in chapter 9, negotiates his internalized oppression as a black man on the "down low." In chapter 10, cultural issues, rooted in age differences, complicate the friendship between two women; students who read this case are challenged to consider cohort differences in working with GLBT people.

1

PASSAGES: FROM FEELING WOMAN TO BEING WOMAN

Stephen Erich, Sandra Donnelly, and Josephine Tittsworth

A STUDENT knocked on the office door of one of the authors not too long ago. She introduced herself as Judy and stated that she wanted to enter the BSW program. They talked about everything necessary to prepare an application packet for review by the BSW Admissions Committee. Judy appeared excited about the opportunity to enter the program. They talked for quite a while, and then Judy informed the professor that she was a transgender individual. The professor believed that it was important to affirm her value as a person, and they began to talk in more detail about her adult life experiences as a 50-year-old postsurgical reassignment surgery transsexual. What follows is her story.

Expressing my feelings is difficult for me. Many instances in my life have caused me such great pain that I have learned to shield myself from the outside world.

I have spent all of my adult life as a cross-dresser. I found it satisfying to wear women's clothes and to portray myself as a woman. The inner feelings related to wearing women's clothes were so strong and unrelentingly forceful that I have always been compelled to seek satisfaction as a woman. This satisfaction is not a need for sexual gratification but a need for self-fulfillment.

I began hormone replacement therapy in 1995. My breasts began to enlarge shortly thereafter. My genitals began to atrophy, and function became impaired. It has been difficult adjusting to the lack of sexual desires. I continued to feel the need to express myself as a woman, but I was also afraid to make the actual commitment to saying I was a woman. The desires to be a woman were slowly surfacing, but I was still in denial.

Medical retirement, in 1999, allowed me an opportunity to live my life full-time as a woman. I could never have taken that step otherwise, due to the fear of losing my financial security. Retirement offered me the opportunity to pursue my dreams. Slowly I started spending more time cross-dressed as a woman. I felt that if living full-time as a woman was what I really wanted, then I needed to experience it as just that. This was a gradual transition in the beginning. I was fearful of how I would be accepted or tolerated in mainstream society.

By the end of the year 2000, I was living as a woman almost all of the time. However, I still had not discussed my cross-dressing with my family—my father, sister, or ex-wife. The only family member who knew anything was my 20-year-old daughter. She knew only that her daddy had been cross-dressing for most of his life.

I felt that I should seek out counseling. I knew that finding a qualified counselor was going to be very difficult. The initial counselor I found was completely clueless about transgenderism. After seeing him weekly for six months, I realized he was not going to help me at all, and I quit therapy.

I finally went to a counselor who was known to have a clear understanding of transgenderism. She was very helpful to me. Through her, I was able to piece together events in my life that had confused me. For example, when I was a teenager, my sister was getting her hair bleached. I was fascinated with this process. I asked my mother to bleach mine also. I felt so great with bleached hair until I went to school the next day and the kids at school ridiculed me relentlessly. Another time while I was in high school, I wanted to take a Homemaking class. The school officials refused to let me because only girls did that. Well, the truth was that I wanted to be with the girls anyway. Even when I was a small child, I liked girls when boys would normally dislike girls. I wanted to be accepted by girls all my life. Therapy allowed me to piece these things together in such a way that I was able to make sense of it all.

In December 2002, I had satisfied all the requirements of the Benjamin Standards of Care (Harry Benjamin International Gender Dysphoria Association, 2001). These requirements are necessary in order to get the green light for sex reassignment surgery (SRS). A qualified therapist, a psychiatrist, and an endocrinologist had treated me and supported my wish to have SRS. I had already completed the requirements of having my name and gender marker legally changed. I had already been living full-time as a woman for two years. At the suggestion of my therapist, I had made sure my entire family was aware of my decision to have a sex change operation.

Dealing with my family was the most difficult part. My feelings of fear and anxiety were intense. My daughter initially became frantic when I told her, but later she calmed down. My father still refuses to acknowledge the change in my life. My sister is trying to adapt, but she still is having trouble with it. All three family members told me that if I want to maintain a relationship with them, I must not allow them to see me as a woman. This saddens me, but I love my family and I am willing to sacrifice in order to keep a relationship. I still hold out [the hope] that someday my family will allow me to be totally who I am today.

The night before my surgery I was scared and still unsure of my decision to continue. A nurse who was also transgendered came to me to help me adjust to what was to come. That night I undressed and stood before a mirror. I looked at my genitalia and contemplated whether or not to proceed. Was this what I wanted? The answer was a resounding "yes." I lay in bed that night again wondering if I should get up and walk out of the hospital. After surgery there would be no changing back ever again. This was to be a permanent change for me.

I closed my eyes and decided that what was to come was meant to be. The next morning I was taken into the operating room, where I spent ten hours while the plastic surgeon performed reconstructive surgery on me. When I awoke, I knew that I could no longer have second thoughts. I was still scared but hopeful.

While in my room, I was fretting over the tube in my nose and all the other attachments around me. These sights alone were depressing. I was not allowed to eat or drink for five days. When each attachment was removed, I felt a sense of great relief.

During this time, I would continually reach down between my legs and feel for what was not there. Today, I still do this. Maybe someday I will fully realize that my male genitalia no longer exist.

I struggled in the hospital due to kidney failure. I went into a state of chemical depression. This was very scary to me. I began to wonder if the surgery was really worth it. I wanted to close my eyes and wish it all away. I had never felt so desperate before in my life. Thankfully, this did not last. After about two weeks, my kidney functions began to return and I was feeling like the same person I have always been.

When I returned home I was still very weak. My ex-wife would come over every day to take care of me. I will be forever grateful to her for that. For a long time, I would not look into the mirror for fear of what I would see. This was a hurdle that I needed to overcome. I found it difficult to look at myself. After about four weeks, I finally started to allow myself to see what I looked like without male genitalia. At first it was startling, but as time went on, I grew to appreciate my new body. I am still fascinated with my appearance in the mirror. Since the final part of the SRS surgery only occurred a few weeks ago, I am still swollen up and I do not want to see it yet. I am still afraid to look.

I still find it difficult at times to refer to myself as a woman, since I spent the largest part of my life declaring myself a man. The assimilation into womanhood is going to be a long and interesting adventure for me. I was conditioned to be male all my life. After beginning to realize that I am actually a woman, I still find it difficult at times to distinguish between the male conditioning and the female within me.

CORRESPONDING TEXTBOOK CHAPTERS

Chapter 5: Transgender identity, by J. I. Martin & D. R. Yonkin.

Chapter 7: Psychosocial support for families of gay, lesbian, bisexual, and transgender people, by H. L. Cohen, Y. C. Padilla, & V. C. Aravena.

Chapter 12: Transgender emergence within families, by A. I. Lev.

ADDITIONAL READINGS

Burke, P. (1996). *Gender shock: Exploding the myths of male and female*. New York: Anchor Books.

Gagne, P., Tewksbury, P., & McGoughey, D. (1997). Coming out and crossing over: Identity formation and proclamation in a transgender community. *Gender and Society, 1*, 478–508.

Harry Benjamin International Gender Dysphoria Association. (2001). *Standards of care for gender identity disorders* (6th version). Minneapolis, MN. Author.

MacKenzie, G. (1994). *Transgender nation*. Bowling Green, OH: Bowling Green State University Popular Press.

Miller, N. (1996). *Counseling in genderland: A guide for you and your transgendered client*. Boston: Different Path Press.

Monro, S. (2000). Theorizing transgender diversity: Towards a social model of health. *Sexual Relationship Therapy, 15*, 33–45.

Rudd, P. (1990). *Crossdressing with dignity: The case of transcending gender lines*. Katy, TX: PM Publishers.

—. (1995). *Crossdressers: And those who share their lives*. Katy, TX: PM Publishers.

—. (1998). *Who's really from Venus? The tale of two genders*. Katy, TX: PM Publishers.

QUESTIONS FOR DISCUSSION

1. What are the acceptable terms for people in the transgender community? What do these terms tell us about the lifestyles and/or characteristics of people in the transgender community?

2. How do female and male socialization processes in the United States affect people from the transgender community? More specifically, how do they affect those people who have completed sex reassignment surgery?

3. What are the requirements of the Benjamin Guidelines for sex reassignment surgery?

4. Identify the types, intensity, and/or combination of feelings that people in the transgender community may experience. Do the same for transgender people who have had sex reassignment surgery.

5. How are the issues faced by transgender people alike and different from those of the gay, lesbian, and bisexual community?

6. How would a transgender person fare in your social work program and in your university?

EXERCISES

EXERCISE 1

Name: Safe Zone Program Exercise

Purpose: To have students become familiar with the idea of "Safe Zone" programs, their intent, various structures, effectiveness, and availability

Structure: Small groups of three or four students conduct specific research assignments before coming to class and report their findings to classmates for further discussion.

Implementation: If your school has a Safe Zone program in place, one group of students will research the university "Safe Zone" program: its guidelines for membership, its use, and its effectiveness. Other student groups will find guidelines for Safe Zone programs from other universities. The groups will report their findings to the larger class, and the larger class will discuss similarities and differences between different models. If your school does not have a Safe Zone program, explore the possibility of implementing such a program at your university.

Suggested Social Work Courses: Human behavior in the social environment (HBSE); diversity courses; practice courses

Suggested Class Size: 15–25

Materials and Time: Access to the Internet. Time needed can vary between 20 and 45 minutes, depending on whether the instructor includes discussion of creating a program.

EXERCISE 2

Name: Transgender Role-Plays

Purpose: To help students become aware of the affective, cognitive, behavioral, and social issues often associated with being a member of the transgender community

Structure: Small groups of three to five students role-play different scenarios, followed by discussion.

Implementation: Students will be divided into teams/groups. They will choose one of the following scenarios or suggest one of their own:

- telling an employer and fellow worker that you will be coming to work as a woman from this day forward;
- telling your minister, priest, rabbi, or other religious leader about your plans to have sex reassignment surgery;
- telling your children, parents, and/or siblings that you are transgender and will be undergoing SRS;
- asking for advice from a friend about how to dress, use makeup, and otherwise carry yourself as a woman.

Once a scenario has been chosen, students in each group will identify which character each of them will play (5 minutes). Student teams/groups will then take turns acting out these scenarios (40–50 minutes). After a team/group is finished, the other classmates and the actors will discuss issues related to feelings, coming out, and implications for social work practice (20 minutes).

Suggested Social Work Courses: HBSE; diversity course; practice courses

Suggested Class Size: 15–25

Materials and Time: No specific materials are required. This exercise takes one class period.

2

FINDING HOPE: THE CASE OF RANDALL

Patricia L. Greer and Deana F. Morrow

RANDALL IS a 19-year-old African American gay man making his first visit to a family services counseling center. The social worker's initial impressions of him are that he is a happy-go-lucky person. He is very bubbly, chatty, friendly, and smiling. Yet, since he is constantly moving and fidgeting, there appears to be an underlying nervousness about him. Once he begins talking about himself, he reveals his story.

Randall starts the conversation by stating that his mother died one year ago today; he laughs nervously as he speaks. Between the ages of 6 and 17, he was in and out of foster care, since it was discovered that his uncle had repeatedly sexually molested him in his mother's home. Even though Randall was placed in foster care, his younger brother was allowed to remain in the home. Randall laughs nervously again as he shares with the worker that he missed growing up with his brother. His mood quickly changes, and he states that he is confused and angry about why he was shunned and removed from his mother's home while his brother was permitted to remain.

Randall returns to the subject of his mother. He laughs while tears well up in his eyes when he says he misses his mother. He describes his mother as a "crack whore" who used some unclean needles and eventually died of AIDS. Her disease was not discovered until she entered a drug treatment program in the year before her death. She and Randall were just getting to know each other again when she became sick and died.

Randall's affect abruptly changes when he says he never knew his father. In a stern, matter-of-fact tone, he states that he did not find out until he was 18 years old that his great-uncle had raped his mother when she was 13 years old. As a result of the rape, she became pregnant and gave birth to Randall. Randall states that he has never had a father figure in his life. The only family male influence he had growing up was the uncle who sexually abused him.

Randall states that he never felt a part of any of the foster homes in which he lived. He says he always felt somewhat like an "alien"—an outsider looking in. There was never any real sense of belonging to any of the families with whom he was placed. His one chance to reconnect with his biological family had been cut short by his mother's death. He reports that his uncle rejected him and sexually abused him for having "gay mannerisms." He reveals that his uncle would call him pejorative names such as "fag" and "swisher" for the way he walked and talked. Consequently, he was also shunned and ridiculed by other members of his biological family, as well as by many of his foster families' siblings, relatives, and friends. Several of the foster families with whom Randall lived were involved in conservative churches. These families would force him to attend church in the hope that he could be changed into a "normal" boy.

As he moved from one foster home to another, Randall went to many different public schools. His school experiences were mostly negative. His schoolmates routinely picked on him and called him such names as "faggot," "queer," and "pervert." On the playground they pushed him down, spat on him, pelted him with rocks and dirt, and ostracized him from playing with other students. In the school restrooms, other boys would urinate on him, shove him into the stalls, and hit him. Randall states that he felt he had no one to rely on for support or guidance in the public schools. The teachers and school administrators ignored his need for support and did nothing to address the inappropriate behaviors of his classmates. Consequently, Randall learned to toughen up and fight as a means of survival. He was suspended on several occasions for fighting, and he eventually dropped out of school when he was 16. He tells the social worker that he is interested in earning a GED but that he is not actively pursuing it.

Poverty is the only condition Randall knows. His biological and foster families were all poor, and there were no real support systems to help him. He angrily states that he is black, gay, and the product of a foster care system where people neither understood nor tried to understand him. Fear, ridicule, rejection, and isolation have been a way of life for Randall.

Randall states that, as a result of his childhood, he has become hardened with regard to life's cruelties. Though he struggled with both external and internal homophobia, he now describes himself as gay and proud. He presently lives with his maternal grandmother and works approximately thirty hours per week cleaning hotel rooms with her. Smiling meekly, Randall states that he doesn't make much money but at least he has a job. He lives in a poor neighborhood and has to ride the bus for transportation. After work he frequently smokes marijuana, which he says helps him cope with life. There is a "drink house" in his neighborhood where illegal alcohol is sold. Even though the house is not licensed to sell alcohol, the residents of the neighborhood know they can get that and more there. Rough people congregate at the drink house, so Randall goes there only when he needs something. He says he enjoys smoking weed and occasionally experiments with other drugs. His smile fades as he states he feels like he is stuck with no way out.

CORRESPONDING TEXTBOOK CHAPTERS

Chapter 3: Oppression, prejudice, and discrimination, by D. E. Elze.
Chapter 8: Gay, lesbian, bisexual, and transgender adolescents, by D. F. Morrow.
Chapter 14: Health concerns for lesbians, gay men, and bisexuals, by C. Ryan & E. Gruskin.
Chapter 16: Violence, hate crimes, and hate language, by M. E. Swigonski.
Chapter 17: Religion and spirituality, by D. F. Morrow & B. Tyson.

ADDITIONAL READINGS

Bourget, S. (2001). Depression: Also known as: "feeling down," "the blues," depressive illness. Retrieved March 6, 2004, from the World Wide Web, http://www.gayhealth.com.
Giddens, S. (1999). *Coping with grieving and loss.* New York: Rosen Publishing Group.
Gilbert, K. R. (1996, May–June). We've had the same loss, why don't we have the same grief? *Death Studies, 20*(3), 269.
Hardin, K. N., & Hall, M. (2001). *Queer blues: The lesbian and gay guide to overcoming depression.* Oakland, CA: New Harbinger Publications.
Jordan, K. M. (2000). Substance abuse among gay, lesbian, bisexual, transgender, and questioning adolescents. *School Psychology Review, 29*(2), 201–207.
Ramirez-Forcier, J. (2003, July 3). Depression and substance abuse. *Gay and Lesbian Times,* 810, 38–40.
Robak, R. W., & Weitzman, S. P. (1998, April–June). The nature of grief: Loss of love relationships in young adulthood. *Journal of Personal and Interpersonal Loss, 3*(2), 205.
Roehr, B. Cope with depression. *Bay Area Reporter.* Retrieved March 6, 2005, from the World Wide Web, http://content.gay.com/channels/health/depression_971022.html.

QUESTIONS FOR DISCUSSION

1. What were some of Randall's strengths?
2. What were his issues?
3. What role does trust play with Randall?
4. Why were Randall's feelings and expressions conflicting with his words?
5. On the basis of Randall's body language and verbal language, what do you think he was feeling as he shared his story?
6. How do you feel about:

- his father/great uncle (who raped his mother)?
- his uncle who sexually abused him?
- his mother?
- his brother?
- Child Welfare Services for removing Randall but not his brother?
- his foster care?
- the religion-based pressure for him to change?
- his classmates in school?
- the school teachers and administrators?

7. Do you think that being sexually abused caused Randall to be gay? Why or why not?

8. If you were gay, how do you think you would feel after hearing this story?

9. Do you think such harsh treatment of gay people by students at school is common? By teachers and administrators?

10. As a social worker, if you heard that this homophobic and hateful treatment had occurred in your local public school district, what would you do?

EXERCISE

Name: Understanding Support Systems

Purpose: To help students identify the many systems that Randall has negotiated and the ways in which those systems help and hinder his progress

Structure: After reading the above case study, the class will divide into groups of four or five students to create an ecomap of the systems Randall has encountered. After they finish their ecomaps, they will gather as a class and discuss them. Finally, the whole class will discuss possible interventions.

Implementation: When students arrive at class, they will have read the case study and will be divided into groups of four or five. One student will be selected to facilitate the group, while another student makes the ecomap (15–20 minutes). When the class regroups, the student taking notes will report a summary of the small-group process (20 minutes). Finally, the groups will discuss how they might intervene to help Randall build on his strengths, address his barriers, and achieve his goals (20 minutes).

Suggested Social Work Courses: This scenario can be used in any social work course that discusses diversity, discrimination, and/or depression and loss.

Suggested Class Size: A minimum of 10 students per class would be best in order to generate discussion.

Materials and Time: Each small group will need an ecomap form with a variety of blank circles/systems. The time needed for successful implementation will be 40–55 minutes.

3

THE COVERT LIFE OF PHILIP JOHNSON

David Henton

PHILIP JOHNSON is a 65-year-old African American male who is seeking clinical social work services from the Houston Community Mental Health Clinic. He initially presents as a successful heterosexual married man. He is recently retired from the Houston Independent School District, where he taught high school math for twenty years. Before beginning his teaching career, Mr. Johnson retired from the U.S. Army as a lieutenant colonel. In his current retirement, he enjoys spending time with his wife of forty-five years, Evelyn Johnson; volunteering in the community; and serving as a deacon in his church and as an officer with the local chapter of the NAACP.

Mr. Johnson was born and raised on a farm in rural east Texas, the eldest of three sons born to Philip and Marvelee Johnson. The senior Mr. Johnson was a farmer and itinerant Baptist preacher. Mrs. Johnson was a homemaker, worked on the farm, and taught Sunday school. The Johnson family was close, including extended-family members throughout the county. Life in the Johnson household revolved around family, church, and the farm. Although they lived a simple and frugal lifestyle, the Johnsons were successful as small farmers and were very well respected in the African American community. Mr. Johnson describes his family of origin as "very loving, but very strict." Children were expected to work hard on the farm and in school, obey their parents, participate in church activities, and respect their elders.

Mr. Johnson's introduction to sexual activity with another male occurred at age 14, when he first engaged in mutual masturbation with a 16-year-old cousin. Over the next four years (until his departure for college), Mr. Johnson continued to engage in significant sexual activity on an ongoing basis, both with his cousin and with several other close male friends. The activity did not include kissing, as that would have been considered "queer"; however, it progressed from mutual masturbation to include both oral and anal intercourse, with Mr. Johnson participating in both active and passive roles. Mr. Johnson describes feeling overwhelming guilt about this covert activity, but he continued to participate in it. He also describes experiencing guilt about masturbating alone, during which times he fantasized primarily about women. Occasional wet dreams were also primarily heterosexual in content. As a result of these heterosexual fantasies and dreams, Mr. Johnson never considered that he might be "queer."

Mr. Johnson began dating heterosexually as soon as he was allowed to do so by his parents, at age 16. He had two fairly serious relationships with high school girlfriends. Although they did not have sexual intercourse, there was significant sexual exploration and an intense emotional connection in both relationships. During both of these relationships, Mr. Johnson's sexual activity with other boys diminished significantly. Mr. Johnson reports that he was much more attracted to his girlfriends than to his male partners and that there was a "passion" in his heterosexual relationships that was lacking in his same-sex activity. Socially, Mr. Johnson was a popular boy in high school, and he enjoyed friendships with both boys and girls.

Although Mr. Johnson vowed to discontinue his sexual activity with other men when he left for college, he soon found himself sexually involved with his freshman roommate, Maurice. Unable to manage the accompanying guilt, and frightened for the first time about his own sexual orientation, Mr. Johnson moved in with a different roommate his sophomore year and finally succeeded in refraining from sexual activity with other men.

Mr. Johnson met Evelyn early in their junior year, and they quickly became inseparable. They were "going steady" within a month of meeting and became sexually active shortly thereafter. Mr. Johnson describes their lovemaking as "incredible" and "unbelievably satisfying." He also describes being deeply in love with his wife, then and now. Mrs. Johnson has been his "soulmate and best friend for forty-five years."

Throughout the first twenty-five years of their life together, Mr. Johnson remained faithful and monogamous in his relationship with his wife. Even during tours of duty in Vietnam and extended absences from his family, Mr. Johnson reports having had little interest in extramarital sexual activity of any kind. Occasional masturbation fantasies were almost exclusively heterosexual, and he rarely thought about his earlier same-sex activity. The Johnsons nurtured their marital relationship despite the challenges of distance, enjoying passionate and intense reunions when they were reunited after each foreign tour of duty. Mr. Johnson considered himself completely heterosexual, fitting in well with the "macho" culture of the military. Despite his love and longing for his wife, Mr. Johnson adjusted well to several all-male assignments: He had good relationships with the other men and enjoyed their camaraderie during furloughs. Although he missed his wife, he was not interested in the company of other women.

During their early forties, the Johnsons experienced several significant changes. Mr. Johnson retired from the army and began teaching. The second of their two children left home for college, and they became "empty nesters." Mrs. Johnson's libido waned significantly, and their sexual activity became increasingly infrequent. Simultaneously, Mr. Johnson began noticing how attractive and appealing young women *and* young men were to him. At first, his attraction to young men seemed "harmless" and asexual to him. For example, in noticing how handsome the 21-year-old son of a longtime neighbor had become, Mr. Johnson remarked to Mrs. Johnson, "That Keith sure has turned out to be a good-looking young man, hasn't he?"

As time and his own middle-aged years progressed, however, Mr. Johnson's attraction to young men became more intense and of a more clearly sexual nature than he had at first understood. In his late forties, Mr. Johnson could no longer deny to himself that he had a significant attraction to young men. During a teachers' conference in Chicago, Mr. Johnson visited a gay bar featuring male strippers. The following year, again during a teachers' conference, Mr. Johnson visited an all-male strip club and found himself exploring the bodies of several of the young dancers, whom he handsomely tipped.

In his early fifties, Mr. Johnson began visiting adult theaters and arcades, where men would sometimes engage in mutual masturbation and/or sex with each other. Although Mr. Johnson initially vowed to himself not to engage in any sexual activity, he soon found himself again engaging in the male-to-male sexual contact he had enjoyed as an adolescent. Although he found the "gay scene" to be highly distasteful, he discovered the existence of gay bathhouses and private clubs where it was possible to engage in anonymous sex, sometimes with much younger men. Throughout his fifties and early sixties, Mr. Johnson thus found himself engaging in considerable covert sexual activity with other men.

Now, at 65, Mr. Johnson is able to acknowledge to himself that he has "significant" attraction to men as well as women. He maintains that he still loves his wife deeply and has no desire to jeopardize their marriage, despite his current risk-taking behavior. Although he and Mrs. Johnson are sexually intimate only infrequently, he worries about contracting and transmitting STDs. He says, "I would just *die* if I ever gave her anything, or if she ever found out about the men." Mr. Johnson also expresses extreme guilt about the disparity between his religious convictions that homosexuality is an "abomination" and his sexual behavior. Furthermore, he is "terrified" that his covert behavior might be discovered by friends or fellow church members.

Currently, Mr. Johnson engages in sexual activity with other men approximately twice a month, usually in a bathhouse or at an adult theater or arcade. He uses condoms and refrains from exchanging bodily fluids. His partners are typically anonymous, and each incident is usually a one-time occurrence. He has periodically traded e-mail addresses and shared repeated encounters with a partner, although the encounters have typically been limited to sexual activity. Mr. Johnson reports no emotional connection with his male sexual partners. He masturbates occasionally and reports both heterosexual and homosexual fantasies in equal intensity; however, the homosexual fantasies tend to involve much younger men exclusively.

Aside from Mrs. Johnson, Mr. Johnson has few female friendships. Most of his close friends are male, and most of his social interaction outside of his marriage is with other men, either individually or in small groups.

Although Mr. Johnson is able to acknowledge to himself that he is attracted to men, he does not consider himself bisexual or gay. In fact, he deeply dislikes both terms. He does not identify with the gay community, and he is deeply ambivalent about his attraction to men and about the compulsive nature of his sexual behavior with them.

CORRESPONDING TEXTBOOK CHAPTERS

Chapter 4: Gay, lesbian, and bisexual identity development, by D. F. Morrow.
Chapter 11: Bisexual relationships and families, by D. L. McClellan.
Chapter 13: Gay, lesbian, bisexual, and transgender older people, by E. M. Fullmer.

ADDITIONAL READINGS

Chung, Y. B., & Katayama, M. (1996). Assessment of sexual orientation in lesbian/gay/bisexual studies. *Journal of Homosexuality*, 30(4), 49–62.
Davis, C. M., Yarber, W. L., Bauserman, R., Schreer, G., & Davis, S. L. (1997). *Handbook of sexuality-related measures.* Thousand Oaks, CA: Sage.
Kinsey, A. C., Pomeroy, W. B., & Martin, C. E. (1998). *Sexual behavior in the human male.* Bloomington: Indiana University Press.
Klein, F. (1993). *The bisexual option* (2nd ed.). New York: Haworth.
Klein, F., & Schwartz, T. (2001). *Bisexual and gay husbands: Their stories, their words.* New York: Haworth.
Sell, R. L. (1997). Defining and measuring sexual orientation: A review. *Archives of Sexual Behavior*, 26(6), 643–658.

QUESTIONS FOR DISCUSSION

1. Some research in human sexuality suggests that adolescent sexual behavior has a profound impact on our subsequent psychosexual identity as adults. Do you agree or disagree with this statement? Why? How might it inform our understanding of Mr. Johnson's current sexual identity?

2. How does Mr. Johnson's ethnic and cultural identity affect his sexual identity? How does his sexual identity affect his cultural identity?

3. Some research in sexual orientation is posited on the grounds that sexual orientation is defined exclusively through sexual attraction, behavior, and fantasies (Kinsey, Pomeroy, & Martin, 1998). Other researchers have argued that sexual orientation is a "dynamic, multi-variable process" including social and emotional preference, self-identity, and lifestyle orientation, in addition to sexual attraction, behavior, and fantasies (Klein, 1993). Which view most closely approximates your own? Why?

4. Does sexual orientation change over time or is it typically a "fixed," static aspect of our nature?

EXERCISE

Name: The Life Span Perspective and Measures of Sexual Orientation.

Purpose: To have students evaluate measures of sexual orientation and affectional preference

Structure: Students will work in three small groups of four to seven students each, with each group examining Mr. Johnson's sexual orientation at a particular time in his life.

Implementation: Students will be randomly assigned to one of the three groups. Each group will select a scribe and a reporter. Each group is charged with examining Mr. Johnson's life at one of three different ages: 18, 35, or 65. Each group will complete the Kinsey Scale, the Klein Sexual Orientation Grid, and the Shively/DeCecco Scale for the age assigned to their group. (Note: Additional measures of sexual orientation, as found in the above references, can also be incorporated into this exercise. The exercise can also be completed as an individual activity or a homework assignment.) The class will then reconvene and hear from each group in chronological order.

Suggested Social Work Courses: Micro practice; HBSE/human development; human sexuality; mental health/diagnostic assessment; research (practice evaluation and/or clinical measurement)

Suggested Class Size: Optimal size is 12–21 students.

Materials and Time: No materials are needed. The time required is 45–60 minutes.

4

BRIAN AT THE CROSSROADS: A CASE STUDY

Sello Sithole

BACKGROUND

Brian is a 29-year-old black man who works as an accounting clerk for a life insurance company in South Africa, in a rural town called Thohoyandou. Over the last few weeks he has been increasingly depressed. He has started drinking excessively until late at night. Because of problems with his finances, his company-sponsored vehicle has been repossessed. Brian's productivity at work also has been declining rapidly over the last few weeks. The last straw, however, was when his fiancée, Mashudu, came into the workplace shouting. She threatened Brian with leaving their child in his office if he failed to provide money for support within the following two days. Her scene caused severe embarrassment to Brian, who was aware that a number of clients and coworkers were noticing this unacceptable behavior in the workplace.

This event prompted Joel Baloyi, the department manager, to summon Brian to his office. Joel raised concerns about the fact that Brian had lost his car because he could not keep up with the installment payments. The loss of his car in turn resulted in Brian's failing to attain his daily and weekly targets. Joel advised Brian to seek counseling from the company's Employee Assistance Program provider. Brian was given a toll-free number to contact a social worker who was contracted to this EAP provider. He went back to his office, made the call, and scheduled an appointment at the social worker's office.

MEETING WITH THE SOCIAL WORKER

The social worker, Rebone Thuso, introduced himself and offered Brian a chair. Brian also introduced himself. Rebone could sense some anxiety and dismissed this as typical of clients at case presentation. He asked what he could do for Brian. Brian laid out the situation as he saw it: he was depressed, his drinking had reached unacceptable levels, his car had been repossessed, his productivity had declined drastically, and his libidinal energy was at its lowest. To top it all off, his fiancée, Mashudu, had created a terrible scene at his workplace, threatening to leave the baby in his office if he did not give her $500 Rand within two days to provide for the child. He explained that he felt overwhelmed by all of these issues and needed some help getting his life in order.

Rebone explained that the approach used in all EAP services was brief therapy, where he and Brian would work on solution plans. As a first step, he asked Brian to prioritize his problems and generate alternatives to address them.

Brian said his priority was to stop Mashudu from coming to his workplace to embarrass him in front of his colleagues and superiors. Brian and Rebone identified an alternative, to set up a meeting with Brian's fiancée to obtain her side of the story, so far as the child's maintenance was concerned, and to negotiate some resolution. Brian's second goal was to get his car back so that he could use it to fulfill his contractual obligations with his employer and reach his potential clients, thereby restoring his productivity. To help Brian meet this goal, Rebone referred him to the legal and financial services within the EAP provider's network of services.

When Rebone asked whether these were all of the problems for which Brian was seeking assistance, Brian's response was noncommittal. He then revealed that he was not sure that he was the baby's father. The social worker requested that he disclose what prompted him to doubt his paternity of the child. Brian confided that his fiancée had been unfaithful to him. When asked whether they had ever talked about this problem, Brian's response was that Mashudu was always denying being unfaithful. Brian reacted positively to the social worker's question as to whether he would be prepared to go for a paternity test. The social worker provided Brian with details of where the tests could be done and how much it would cost him.

However, since Brian still seemed to be dissatisfied, Rebone verbalized his observations of Brian's body language. In response, Brian said that he had a problem with his identity. Rebone asked him to explain what he meant by that, since the concept of identity is extremely broad. Brian ultimately provided the social worker with a window to his past.

Brian mentioned that he had completed his high school education at a boys' high school, where he had realized that he was attracted to his male friends. He actually went on to say that he had several sexual relationships with male friends then. He nevertheless revealed that he was attracted to women as well, though his attraction to women was less intense.

The need to establish a family and have children was also a burning desire for Brian, despite having a male sex partner in Cape Town. His male lover wanted Brian to join him so that they could share a flat and live together as partners. Rebone asked Brian if he did not want to live with his lover, but Brian said this would delay his plans for getting married.

After a lengthy discussion, Brian asked Rebone whether it could work to have both a heterosexual and a homosexual relationship simultaneously. The social worker's response was that Mashudu would probably discover that Brian had another relationship and this could cause severe resentment on her part. What would probably be most appropriate in such a situation would be for a person to make his own choices in life. Rebone assured Brian that it was not his duty or intention to suggest moral prescriptions for Brian's lifestyle. The social worker also acknowledged that it was his first encounter with bisexuality. Because Rebone felt inadequate to deal with the situation at hand, he asked Brian to give him a chance to do further reading on the subject so that he could maximize his assistance.

Brian agreed to Rebone's proposal and confirmed that he had never before "come out" to a stranger about his dual sexuality. Rebone was the first person in whom he had confided, and he asked for confidentiality.

Rebone reassured Brian of his ethical principles, particularly concerning confidentiality. Brian made a further request that his sexuality should not surface at the social worker's meeting with Mashudu. Rebone assured him once more that it would not happen.

Rebone ended the session by expressing his appreciation of the fact that Brian had decided to come out to him. He also expressed his own disappointment with his inability to provide immediate answers to some of the challenging questions that Brian raised. They scheduled an appointment for the next session.

AFTERWORD

Rebone immediately took the opportunity to obtain more information about the sexuality issues that Brian raised. He borrowed books from the library, started discussing these issues with colleagues, and discovered the limitations of his own training and experiences. The literature and Internet search exposed the social worker's ignorance about GLBT people.

When Brian came for the second interview, Rebone provided him with all the Web sites he had found that related to GLBT people. He also expressed disappointment at the unavailability of resources for GLBT people in their small town. Brian responded that he appreciated the social worker's efforts, but he indicated that his problem about identity remained unresolved. At this stage, Rebone told Brian that he was unable to offer further assistance for solving Brian's problem and referred him to a psychologist who had in-depth knowledge about sexual identity and GLBT people.

CORRESPONDING TEXTBOOK CHAPTERS

Chapter 4: Gay, lesbian, and bisexual identity development, by D. F. Morrow.
Chapter 11: Bisexual relationships and families, by D. L. McClellan.

ADDITIONAL READINGS

Alexander, J. (2002). "Behind the Mask": An African gay-affirmative website. *International Journal of Sexuality and Gender Studies, 7*(2–3), 227–234.
Rust, P. C. (2001). Two many and not enough: The meanings of bisexual identities. *Journal of Bisexuality, 1*(1), 31–68.
Stokes, J. P., Damon, W., & McKirnan, D. J. (1997). Predictors of movement toward homosexuality: A longitudinal study of bisexual men. *Journal of Sex Research, 34*(3), 304–312.

QUESTIONS FOR DISCUSSION

1. Do you regard the social worker's knowledge about GLBT people as sufficient for the level at which he had to function?

2. Do you think the social worker succeeded in winning Brian's confidence from the beginning of the interview?

3. Did the social worker demonstrate appropriate valued-guided behavior?

4. Did you sense some homophobic tendencies from the social worker?

5. If you were in the position of the social worker, how would you handle this problem?

6. How should the social worker go about increasing his understanding and appreciation of GLBT people?

7. Interpret Brian's behavior in terms of Erik Erikson's stages of psychosexual development. How does this relate to Brian's stage of identity development?

8. If you were the manager of the insurance company where Brian worked, what would you do for employees who were experiencing problems such as his? If you were the chief executive officer of this company, what would you do to sensitize the workforce about GLBT people?

EXERCISE

Name: The Nature/Nurture Debate

Purpose: To familiarize the students with the intricacies of arguments regarding human sexuality

Structure: At the end of one class, six to ten students will be randomly assigned to four groups. The first two groups will speak for or against the statement "Homosexuality is caused by nature." The third group of students (and perhaps outsiders) will be designated as judges, and the remaining students will serve as audience. This fourth group will select a chairperson to facilitate the debate. Students will need time outside of class to prepare their arguments and marshal their resources as a group.

Implementation: The first person to deliver his/her presentation will be from the affirmative group, followed by a student from the negative group. That order should be maintained until the last student has presented. Each student will have 10–15 minutes to deliver his/her presentation. The panel of judges will allocate marks or give prizes to the two groups. If possible, the judges should include GLBT people from the class or the larger community. After the presentations, the judges will confer and then critique the arguments on both sides. The chairperson may pronounce a verdict (who won) on the basis of submissions from the panel of judges.

Suggested Class Size: No fewer than 15, possibly as many as 35

Materials and Time: 75–90 minutes

5

YOUNG, TRANSGENDER, AND OUT IN EAST LOS ANGELES

David Henton

JUANITA RAMIREZ is a 17-year-old transgender Latina. The youngest of eight children, Juanita was born and raised as Juan in East Los Angeles. Juanita's parents, Jose and Guadalupe, immigrated to the United States from Oaxaca, Mexico, as teenagers. Jose has an eighth-grade education and works as a truck driver. Guadalupe ("Lupe") has a fourth-grade education and is a homemaker. Both parents and all the children are bilingual, although Spanish is the primary language spoken in the home. The Ramirezes are of the working class and traditional in their attitudes about gender roles. They maintain close ties with both of their families in Oaxaca. The Ramirezes are Catholic, but only Lupe practices the faith on a regular basis. In addition to her immediate family, Juanita has numerous aunts, uncles, and cousins, both in Southern California and in Oaxaca.

From earliest childhood Juanita played with other girls. Growing up, she always preferred the company of the women in her family. Her youngest sibling, her sister Rosita, who is two years older than Juanita, always treated Juanita as her baby sister. As a child, Juanita enjoyed cooking and visiting with her mother and her *tias* (aunts) and never expressed any interest in socializing or working with the men in her family. The women in Juanita's family accepted her presence with them unquestioningly. However, it was always a source of conflict between Juanita and her father, who worried about his son being a "sissy" and frequently berated him for his rejection of traditionally masculine gender roles.

From an early age Juanita was teased in school, initially as a "sissy" and a "momma's boy," and later on as a "faggot" and a "*joto.*" Although she always had several close girlfriends and enjoyed playing with other girls as a child, the taunting of boys in her classes grew more problematic in adolescence. In both the ninth and the tenth grades, Juanita was assaulted at school by male classmates. Although the assaults occurred on school property and during regular class hours, school officials never investigated or pursued Juanita's assailants. Although she was an A student and excelled in school, Juanita dropped out at age 16 because of the harassment she was experiencing from male classmates.

Juanita initially came out as "gay" to herself, several girlfriends, and her sister Rosita at age 13. All of these initial experiences with coming out were positive. At age 14, she came out to her parents. Her mother responded by assuring Juanita of her love but also promising to pray for her "to be normal." Her father was furious and kicked Juanita out of the home, over the protests of Juanita's mother and Rosita. Juanita then lived with several girlfriends on a temporary basis. After appeals from his wife and Rosita, Juanita's father relented and allowed her to return home. However, after she began openly dressing and living as a girl, Juanita's father again kicked her out of the home. Juanita then moved in with her *tia* Concepción and her four young children. Concepción's home was crowded, however, and Juanita's presence became a stressor for the household. Juanita eventually wound up living with a distant cousin, Marta, and her lesbian partner, Becky, in their home in an affluent suburban community. Juanita's growing flamboyance soon made Marta and Becky increasingly uncomfortable in their relationship with their neighbors. When they asked Juanita to move out, she was again forced to seek temporary refuge with girlfriends.

Shortly after she began dressing and living as a girl in public, Juanita began "dating" guys she met on the street outside (and occasionally inside) bars. Although she does not consider these dates to be prostitution, she has in fact dated men for money on a number of occasions. Typically these dates culminate in her performing oral sex on her date. Twice she has been assaulted by men who discovered that she was not biologically female. In one incident she sustained only minor injuries; in the other she was raped and required medical attention in the hospital emergency room. Although she was treated for a concussion and a broken jaw, she did not disclose the rape to emergency room personnel and was never treated for rectal bleeding, which she experienced at the time.

Currently, Juanita is living with her girlfriend Isabel, who is also a transgender Latina. Juanita primarily relies on Isabel and other friends in meeting her basic needs. She does occasionally receive money from "dates." She also receives some occasional assistance from Rosita and from their mother.

Juanita is unemployed and has a very limited work history, having sometimes worked in fast-food restaurants for short periods of time. She would like to finish her GED and find a good-paying job. She would also like to meet "the right man" and form a long-term relationship. Her expectations, for both employment and romantic engagement, are immediate and unrealistic.

Juanita lives as a woman and considers herself to be female. She wants to begin hormone therapy and eventually have sex reassignment surgery. Although she remains biologically male, Juanita has a good self-image. She is proud of "being able to pass," a consequence of her sparse facial hair, feminine voice and mannerisms, petite build, and soft facial features.

Juanita appears to be in good health, although she has received no medical attention in the past four years other than her single visit to the emergency room. She smokes marijuana several times a week and occasionally uses other recreational drugs (ecstasy and cocaine). She drinks alcohol about twice a month when she and friends are able to get it. Her drinking on those occasions is sometimes excessive and ends in her passing out.

Juanita enjoys dancing, roller-skating, cooking, eating, and "hanging out with friends." Despite her youth, she is occasionally able to get into clubs, where she also enjoys entertaining as an amateur drag artist. She continues to maintain a close relationship with her sister Rosita and, to a lesser extent, her mother, Concepción, and several other *tias*. She has no relationship with her father or other men in her family and is able to visit her mother's home only when her father is on the road.

CORRESPONDING TEXTBOOK CHAPTERS

Chapter 5: Transgender identity, by J. I. Martin & D. R. Yonkin.

Chapter 7: Psychosocial support for families of gay, lesbian, bisexual, and transgender people, by H. L. Cohen, Y. C. Padilla, & V. C. Aravena.

Chapter 8: Gay, lesbian, bisexual, and transgender adolescents, by D. F. Morrow.

ADDITIONAL READINGS

Atkins, D. (1998). *Looking queer: Body image and identity in lesbian, bisexual, gay, and transgender communities*. New York: Haworth.

Boschenek, M., & Brown, A. W. (2001). *Hatred in the hallways: Violence and discrimination against lesbian, gay, bisexual, and transgender students in U.S. schools*. New York: Human Rights Watch.

Finnegan, D. G., & McNally, E. B. (2002). *Counseling lesbian, gay, bisexual, and transgender substance abusers: Dual identities*. New York: Haworth.

Gay and Lesbian Medical Association. (2001). *Healthy people 2010: Companion document for gay, lesbian, bisexual, and transgender (GLBT) health*. San Francisco: Gay and Lesbian Medical Association.

Israel G. E., & Tarver, D. E. (1997). *Transgender care: Recommended guidelines, practical information, and personal accounts*. Philadelphia: Temple University Press.

National Latino/a Lesbian and Gay Organization. (1995). *La guia: A resource guide for lesbian, gay, bisexual, and transgender Latinos*. Washington, DC: National Latino/a Lesbian and Gay Organization.

U.S. Department of Health and Human Services. (2001). *A provider's introduction to substance abuse treatment for lesbian, gay, bisexual, and transgender individuals*. Rockville, MD: Center for Substance Abuse Treatment, Substance Abuse and Mental Health Services Administration, U.S. Department of Health and Human Services.

QUESTIONS FOR DISCUSSION

1. What are Juanita's current strengths and needs?

2. Is Juanita's experience with coming out first as "gay" and only later identifying as transgender typical or atypical? Why?

3. What resources does Juanita have in her current environment? What barriers does she encounter?

4. You are an intake social worker in a social service agency providing services to GLBT youth. How will you build rapport with Juanita? Think about your own gender, sexual orientation, and gender identity. How might your self-identity affect your work with Juanita?

5. Given Juanita's various concerns, where would you begin your work with her?

EXERCISE

Name: Assessment and Case Planning with a Transgender Client

Purpose: To have students develop a psychosocial assessment and intervention plan for a transgender client

Structure: Students will work in three to four small groups of four to seven students each. The class will then reconvene and hear from each group. Classroom discussion will address similarities and differences between the groups' assessments and intervention plans.

Implementation: Students are randomly assigned to small groups. Each group selects a scribe and a reporter. Students are instructed to: (a) identify Juanita's strengths and needs; (b) develop an intervention plan with goals, objectives, and outcome measures; (c) identify appropriate referrals; and (d) identify evaluation criteria. Students may also complete an ecomap, a time line, and/or a genogram—as part of this exercise, as a preparatory homework assignment before this exercise, or as a second small-group exercise.

Suggested Social Work Courses: Micro practice; HBSE; family practice

Suggested Class Size: 12–28

Materials and Time: Posterboard paper and markers for recording. The exercise will take 60–90 minutes.

6

THE MILITARY LIFE: THE CASE OF SAUNDRA

Patricia L. Greer and Deana F. Morrow

SAUNDRA IS a 44-year-old African American lesbian who grew up in a New York City housing project. Her parents divorced when she was very young. She remained with her mother while her father moved to South Carolina. Saundra had no virtually contact with her father until she became an adult and reached out to him. Her mother worked inconsistently and was neglectful of her children. Saundra took on the responsibility of caring for herself and her two younger siblings. They had to scrape by to get food and stay safe in their run-down environment. Thus, from early in life, Saundra had to learn to be resourceful and survive.

By the tenth grade, Saundra realized she was a lesbian. She was never interested in boys; instead, she felt attracted to girls. She had a secret crush on another girl in high school, but knowing the importance of surviving in her world, she did not act upon her feelings. Life was tough for Saundra. She dropped out of high school at age 16. Once out of school, she began going to gay bars in order to socialize with other young women like her. She had a series of relationships with various other women that she described as "serial monogamy." These relationships were neither long term nor particularly meaningful for Saundra.

By the mid-1970s, when Saundra was 19 years old, she had had enough and wanted to get away. She decided to join the air force. Though she was intelligent, Saundra had rarely applied herself in school, but she would have to complete the GED in order to be eligible to enlist. She hesitatingly signed up for the test and was both surprised and pleased when she passed. This achievement was the boost she needed. She realized that she was smarter than she had given herself credit for and could accomplish positive things in life rather than repeating the existence her mother had lived.

Once in the air force, Saundra learned she had to toughen up in order to survive. Basic training challenged her to excel. She was enthralled with the structure and discipline that the air force gave her—something she had never had as a child. With this realization, she submerged herself in learning all she could in order to succeed in the military. This new life was in stark contrast to her upbringing, and she thrived. During her eighteen-year military career Saundra was stationed at several bases around the United States and in Germany. She appreciated that the military gave her the opportunity to see parts of the world she otherwise would have only dreamed of seeing.

Because of the military's discriminatory policies against lesbians and gays, Saundra knew she must keep her sexual orientation a secret. She had witnessed how other lesbians and gays had been shunned and discharged from the military, and she knew that being open about her sexual orientation would result in the termination of her military career. During her first five years in the service, she became something of a workaholic and tended to avoid socializing. Her niche was as a military police officer (MP) in the air force, and she did not want anything to jeopardize this career. To be a team player and fit in was of utmost importance in order to remain in good standing with her military peers and superiors. Implementation of the "don't ask, don't tell" policy in 1993 meant a heightened threat of exposure for lesbians and gays. Discharges from the military increased dramatically. Saundra was well aware of the possibility of witch-hunts, investigations, harassment, torture, and death threats that faced anyone in the military who was even perceived to be lesbian or gay.

As an MP, Saundra learned to be loud, assertive, and spunky. She knew how to play the games, jump through the right hoops, and put on her "military face." However, the years of social isolation took a toll on her. She became more reclusive and awkward around others when she was not on duty. She felt like she had lost a part of herself and desperately wanted to find it. On the one hand, the air force had molded her and conditioned her to act as a proper MP. On the other hand, she slowly suffocated under the mask of "don't ask, don't tell." Saundra felt increasingly desperate to socialize with other women like herself. She decided to go to gay bars in nearby cities away from the military base. On these occasions she was able to relax and be herself—to reconnect with a part of herself that had been buried under her military persona and the fear of exposure and early (possibly dishonorable) discharge. Saundra knew she was taking a huge risk by going to gay bars, but she needed an outlet to meet other lesbians and to be true to herself. Because of her fear of public exposure, however, she kept relationships primarily on a superficial level. From the time of her childhood into adulthood, she had learned to keep an emotionally safe distance between herself and others. Serial monogamy with women once again became a way of life for Saundra.

After eighteen years of service, Saundra was honorably discharged from the air force. Unsure where to go next, she enrolled in a community college, but she did not finish her degree. She also continued her pattern of serial monogamous relationships. This pattern of avoiding deep emotional involvement is persisting, well after her discharge from the air force.

CORRESPONDING TEXTBOOK CHAPTERS

Chapter 3: Oppression, prejudice, and discrimination, by D. Elze.
Chapter 18: Workplace issues, by K. M. Hash.
Chapter 19: Social welfare policy and advocacy, by L. Messinger.

ADDITIONAL READINGS

Belkin, A. (2001). The Pentagon's gay ban is not based on military necessity. *Journal of Homosexuality, 41*(1), 103–120.

Bull, C. (2001, July 17). Barry Winchell's legacy. *Advocate, 842*, 25–28.

Herek, G. M., Jobe, J. B., & Carney, R. M. (Eds.). (1996). *Out in force: Sexual orientation and the military.* Chicago: University of Chicago Press.

Katzenstein, M. F., & Reppy, J. (Eds.). (1999). *Beyond zero tolerance: Discrimination in the military culture.* Lanham, MD: Rowman and Littlefield.

Kirby, D. (2001, May 8). Another soldier's story. *Advocate, 837*, 26–29.

Lehring, G. L. (2003). *Officially gay: The political construction of sexuality by the U.S. military.* Philadelphia: Temple University Press.

Planck, C. (2001, December). Still serving in silence. *Lesbian News, 27*(5).

Rimmerman, C. A. (Ed.). (1996). *Gay rights, military wrongs: Political perspectives on lesbians and gays in the military.* New York: Garland.

Webber, W. S. (1993). *Lesbians in the military speak out.* Northboro, MA: Madwoman Press.

QUESTIONS FOR DISCUSSION

1. Because of the United States "don't ask, don't tell" military policy, Saundra became socially isolated in order to keep her sexual orientation secret. What are the potential psychosocial costs of such isolation?

2. Suppose you are a social worker serving in the military and Saundra comes to you for counseling. In working with you, she shares with you that she is a lesbian. Would you disclose that information to your superior officer? How might the NASW *Code of Ethics* influence your actions?

3. How does the "don't ask, don't tell" policy of the military fit with social work values and ethics? In particular, how does it relate to the concept of social justice?

4. What possible actions could be implemented toward changing the "don't ask, don't tell" policy?

EXERCISE

Name: Playing the Role

Purpose: (a) To have students empathize with lesbians in the military, (b) to get reactions from the three students dramatizing this situation, and (c) to have the role-playing students receive feedback from their classmates on how they felt and what they thought about the scenario

Structure: Three students will role-play a scenario, after which the class will discuss it.

Implementation: The students will read the case study before class. In class, the instructor will ask for three volunteers for the scenario. Each student will receive a description of his or her character and the scenario (see character cards and scenario below), all of which will be read aloud to the class. This should take 5 minutes. Students will then present the scenario, which will take 7–10 minutes.

After the presentation, the instructor will ask the students who participated in the activity the following questions (5 minutes):

1. How did you feel while playing your part?
2. What did you like or dislike about your role?
3. What do you think you could have said or done differently?

The instructor will then direct the following questions to the larger class:

1. What were the strengths of the characters?
2. What issues were brought up?
3. What role does trust play with gays and lesbians in the military?
4. What were the conflicts?
5. How were conflicts resolved?
6. What could the three people have done that would have resulted in a different outcome?
7. If you were gay, how would you feel watching this role-play situation?
8. How important is it to follow the rules versus being yourself and being out?
9. Is it fair that lesbians and gays in the military have to choose between the rules or being out to others? Should this change?

This larger discussion will last 30–40 minutes.

Suggested Social Work Courses: Any course that discusses diversity, prejudice, and discrimination.

Suggested Class Size: A minimum of 10 students per class would be best in order to generate discussion. If a class is larger than 15 students, then after the role-playing, students should be divided into small groups of 4 or 5 to facilitate the discussion questions and then reconvene as a large group at the end of 30 minutes for each small group to share highlights of their discussions.

Materials and Time: The three character descriptions should be put on separate pieces of paper or note cards. The exercise will require 45–55 minutes for successful implementation.

7

SHONDA HARRISON: A YOUNG TRANSGENDER CLIENT IN JAIL

Patricia M. Hayes and Robert H. Keefe

SHONDA HARRISON is a 19-year-old African American male-to-female transgender youth. She called the Gay/Lesbian/Bisexual/Transgender Community Center from the local jail asking to speak with the youth worker, Penny Hughes. Penny, a white 28-year-old social worker, spoke with Shonda for several minutes. After she determined that Shonda was not in immediate danger, Penny arranged to meet with her later in the week.

During the meeting, Shonda discloses that she was arrested for prostitution after a local police sting operation and was sent to the county jail. Once the police officers discovered that Shonda was biologically male, she was immediately transferred to the men's unit, where she has been serving her sentence. Shonda states that the time in jail "has been tough." She reports that the guards and inmates have verbally and physically harassed her. Moreover, because she presents physically as female in an all-male jail, she has had to deal with numerous unwanted sexual advances from other jailers. She reports that she has occasionally engaged in sex with older jailers in return for physical protection. She states that the sex has been unprotected because the jail prohibits condom distribution and she is now frightened about contracting sexually transmitted diseases. Although the inmates who have forced themselves upon her sexually have promised to protect her from the other jailers, she has been in several fights, which led the guards to place her in an isolation cell. When her time in isolation was completed, jail administrators decided to keep her in the isolation cell to protect her from the other inmates.

When questioned about her social support system, Shonda states that her family has always been unsupportive of her. She reports that she frequently fought with her mother, who was raising her and her three younger siblings alone. Shonda claims that the fights mostly concerned her cross-dressing and her "faggot friends," of whom her mother did not approve. She states that she was hurt by her mother's callousness and felt that the few friends she had were extremely important to her.

Even with these few friends, Shonda's high school life was worse than her home life. She states that she dropped out of high school in the tenth grade when the harassment from other students became so overwhelming that she felt she could no longer live safely as a female. The teachers were unsupportive, telling Shonda that she should expect her fellow students to ridicule her, given the way she dressed.

Although Shonda has initiated some contact with her mother and siblings, she has not lived at home in more than two years and has often been homeless. Immediately before her arrest, she was living with several other trans youth in a one-bedroom apartment. Shonda has developed a cohesive relationship with her roommates and other trans individuals, and she refers to them as her "sisters" and her "main family."

Shonda's situation is made worse because she does not have a high school diploma and is thus unable to secure employment that provides health insurance. The escalating costs of the medical care she requires in order to transition from male to female have forced her to resort to prostitution. When asked about her use of other social services, Shonda states that her interactions with the medical community have been a nightmare. Because she does not have a permanent address or proper identification, she has had great difficulty in accessing services. When she contacted the Department of Social Services to enroll in Medicaid, she was told that Medicaid would not cover the cost of treatment to begin the process of transitioning from male to female, including hormone treatment and the necessary psychotherapy that follows the Benjamin

Standards. Out of desperation, Shonda decided to approach several local free health clinics, knowing they would not likely be of much help with her unique medical needs. She states that although the clinics' workers were sympathetic toward her, they could provide only basic health services and not the comprehensive treatment she needed. Finally, about a year ago, feeling that she had no other options, she began injecting "street mons" (i.e., black-market hormones), using needles that she shares with her "roommates."

Over the last year of using the black-market hormones, her physical characteristics have gradually changed. Her facial features have begun to "soften" and she has begun to develop breasts. However, upon entering jail, she was not allowed to take the hormones because she did not have a legal prescription for them before she was arrested.

As she talks about her release from jail, Shonda expresses an interest in setting goals for herself. She states that she would like to attain her GED and look for "legitimate" work after her release. She is skeptical about finding adequate health care, however, as employers' health care plans do not cover the treatment she needs in order to transition and she feels that she will probably be forced to continue using black-market hormones. Shonda also states that her housing situation is far too tenuous and will also need to be addressed.

As Penny listened to the issues that Shonda raised, it became clear that both micro and macro concerns needed to be addressed. Knowing that post-release planning would not take place at the jail, Penny met with Shonda several times at the jail to help Shonda figure out how to approach her housing, employment, education, and health care needs. The youth worker contacted various agencies, including the local needle exchange program, the department of education, the county housing office, and the bureau of vocational rehabilitation, to help broker services that Shonda would need upon being released from jail.

Next, in an attempt to address the macro concerns, Penny contacted the local sheriff's department to schedule an appointment with the sheriff to advocate that a liaison from the sheriff's office and the jail to the GLBT community be appointed. Penny asked Shonda to keep a journal of incidents and contacts she made with guards, her fellow inmates, and jail administrators to help her frame the argument for a liaison staff person. Penny obtained permission from Shonda to share parts of the journal with the sheriff's department in an effort to raise awareness of the treatment that transgender people receive while in jail. Finally, Penny asked Shonda to encourage other transgender youth in the jail to call the community center if they too were in need of support and/or help.

These efforts proved fruitful; a staff person was appointed to serve as a liaison between legal officials (i.e., the sheriff's office and the jail) and the local GLBT community. Penny volunteered to provide consultation and training to the liaison and introduce him to the key leaders in the GLBT community.

After the liaison met many of the GLBT community leaders, efforts were redirected to securing a separate unit of the jail to be devoted to GLBT inmates. Penny hit a dead end on this goal. The warden stated that the jail already had a "vulnerable inmates" unit to which GLBT inmates could be assigned. Penny stressed that such units are also reserved for rapists; many transgender people have been victims of sexual abuse, and thus placement in the unit would not be safe for them. The warden informed Penny that he would investigate the possibility of establishing such a unit, but would make no promises.

CORRESPONDING TEXTBOOK CHAPTERS

Chapter 8: Gay, lesbian, bisexual, and transgender adolescents, by D. F. Morrow.
Chapter 15: Transgender health issues, by E. Lombardi & S. M. Davis.

ADDITIONAL READINGS

Broad, K. L. (2002). Fracturing transgender: Intersectional constructions and identization. *Advances in Gender Research*, 6, 235–266.
Clements-Nolle, K., Marx, R., Guzman, R., & Katz, M. (2001). HIV prevalence, risk behaviors, health care use, and mental health status of transgender persons: Implications for public health intervention. *American Journal of Public Health*, 91(6), 915–921.

Cochran, B. N., Stewart, A. J., Ginzler, J. A., & Cause, A.M. (2002). Challenges faced by homeless sexual minorities: Comparison of gay, lesbian, bisexual, and transgender homeless adolescents with their heterosexual counterparts. *American Journal of Public Health, 92*(5), 773–777.

DeLois, K., & Cohan, M. B. (2000). A queer idea: Using group work principles to strengthen learning in a sexual minorities seminar. *Social Work with Groups, 23*(3), 53–67.

Drabble, L. (2000). Alcohol, tobacco, and pharmaceutical industry funding: Considerations for organizations serving lesbian, gay, bisexual, and transgender communities. *Journal of Gay and Lesbian Social Services, 11*(1), 1–26.

Gagne, P., Tewksbury, R., & McGaughey, D. (1997). Coming out and crossing over: Identity formation and proclamation in a transgender community. *Gender and Society, 11*(4), 478–508.

Lombardi, E., Wilchins, R. A., Priesing, D., & Malouf, D. (2001). Gender violence: Transgender experiences with violence and discrimination. *Journal of Homosexuality, 42*(1), 89–101.

QUESTIONS FOR DISCUSSION

1. Many transgender individuals have limited support systems. Consider times in your own life when you felt you were a victim of discrimination or inequality. While reflecting on the feelings you had during these times, consider the following questions: To whom would you turn for help? How would these individuals respond to you? How did your relationship with the people and the other supports you had in your ecosystem evolve over this time? Compare your own experience with Shonda's and think about where you would start in your work with her.

2. Draw an ecomap for Shonda as well as your own ecomap. As you consider the two ecomaps, what do you feel would be the most difficult issues you would have to face in forming a therapeutic relationship with Shonda? How would you address these issues within yourself so that you could develop a successful therapeutic relationship?

3. As a social worker working with the Gay, Lesbian, Bisexual, and Transgender Community Center, and using Shonda's ecomap as a guide, how would you proceed to help Shonda develop her own ecosystem?

4. In your work with Shonda, you decide that the jail guards would benefit from training in transgender cultural competence. What do you anticipate as being the main training issues you would have to address?

5. Most insurance companies will pay only for routine medical services and not the additional services that transgender clients require. As a result, many transgender clients resort to unsafe practices, including prostitution and needle sharing. The insurance companies report that services that follow the Benjamin Standards, such as sex reassignment surgery (SRS), hormone therapy, and psychotherapy, are too expensive. However, some pharmaceutical companies and some service providers report that their overall profits have risen over the past several years. Given this information, discuss why insurance companies should or should not reimburse these medical providers for services.

6. Many former inmates report engaging in unsafe sex practices while incarcerated. How would you develop a policy on condom distribution in jails to prevent the exchange of body fluids? What systems would need to be in place to enforce this policy?

7. What additional policies could be developed in prison that would be sensitive to the needs of transgender clients?

EXERCISE

Name: Making a Difference: Writing a Proposal

Purpose: To provide students with the opportunity to examine critically the process and details needed to develop a successful proposal for the creation of a separate jail unit for incarcerated transgender inmates

Structure: For this group assignment the class will be divided into groups of five students each. Questions that critically examine the details of the proposal for a separate jail unit for transgender inmates will be provided for students to answer. Each question should take the students between 8 and 10 minutes to complete.

Implementation: The students in each group will read the case addendum (below) and the additional questions (below). Each student will adopt the perspective of one of the five stakeholders. A volunteer from the group will take notes, summarizing the group members' responses to each question. The students will spend 8 to 10 minutes discussing their thoughts on each question. The group will select a person (preferably not the transcriber) to read the group's responses, while the instructor summarizes the points on a chalkboard or whiteboard.

Suggested Social Work Courses: Generalist practice classes, particularly mezzo and macro level sections of those courses

Suggested Class Size: The class should have fewer than 25 students to ensure the best opportunity for discussion of each group's responses. More than five groups would take more time than the instructor would likely want to devote to the assignment.

Materials and Time: Students will need pens and paper to write their responses. The instructor will need a chalkboard or whiteboard to summarize the responses from each group. This exercise will require 55–60 minutes.

CASE ADDENDUM

Several days after the meeting, Penny received a telephone call from the warden, who informed her that a separate unit for transgender inmates would not be granted. Although she was disappointed with this decision, Penny was convinced that a unit was indeed necessary, and she began to draft a proposal that she would submit to the warden and the state department of corrections. In order to be successful, Penny realized, she would need to develop a cogent argument and gain the assistance of community stakeholders to help move her efforts forward.

Among the key stakeholders that Penny identified were the presidents of the GLBT community center and the regional chapter of the National Association of Social Workers, the leader of the state GLBT lobby group, a straight ally on the board of county commissioners, and the jail advocate. During a meeting with these representatives, Penny outlined the following issues to be addressed in the proposal:

1. A section of the jail should be set aside for transgender people.
2. Correctional officers and other staff should be trained about the biopsychosocial issues of transgender jail inmates.
3. The jail should develop a mental health program for inmates who need these services and ensure that the unique needs of the transgender inmates are specifically addressed.
4. The jail's medical clinic staff should be required to prove their competence in working with transgender inmates.
5. Access to hormone therapy should be provided through the medical clinic. Access should be granted regardless of whether the hormones were acquired with a physician's prescription.
6. Transgender inmates should be provided with HIV/STD peer education, including condom distribution, that is sensitive to the transgender community.
7. Issues having to do with clothing and strip searches will be addressed. These issues include the policies concerning wearing makeup and feminine clothing, such as bras for those who have developed breasts, as well as the practice of strip searches by male officers. These policies will be evaluated and rewritten.

Using the information above, answer the following questions:

1. What data do you need to make your case to the state department of corrections? Consider how you would use quantitative and qualitative data in determining best practices.
2. What must be included in the training to help the guards, correctional counselors, social service staff, and medical staff become sensitive to the needs of the transgender inmates incarcerated in their particular unit?
3. What does the jail need to do to formalize relationships so that transgender clients obtain the necessary services to promote their transition from their biological sex to the sex with which they identify, if this is their goal?
4. How would you evaluate the success of the program?

8

SANDY MILLER'S COMPETENCY, RELIGIOUS BELIEFS, AND HOMOPHOBIA

Glenda F. Lester Short

THE CLIENT, Julie Rogers, had just revealed that she thought she was a lesbian. Sandy Miller, her social worker, responded, "What do you mean, you think you're a lesbian? You have a husband and a four-year-old daughter." Sandy wondered if she had screamed the words or had merely asked the question calmly. She hoped the latter was true. Her mind was going a mile a minute. *Gay. Lesbian.* Those were just words; she knew they weren't her clients, people she worked with and liked. She thought to herself, "Great. Now what am I supposed to do?"

THE SOCIAL WORKER

Sandy was 38 years old and had completed her master of social work degree three years earlier. She was currently working in an outpatient mental health clinic in a small suburb of a Midwestern city. Her clients were mostly children and parents experiencing child-related school and discipline problems. From time to time Sandy would receive an adult female client who had adjustment issues such as a divorce, the death of an elderly parent, or a recent or unexpected move to a new location.

Sandy was well liked by her clients because she listened attentively and seemed to have their best interests at heart. She was often told, "I feel like you care about me and what happens in my life." The truth was, she did, and it showed. At times she had to advocate for clients, and there was never a more serious advocate. Sandy stood up for the rights of others and empowered them to do the same. Management wasn't always happy with her, but the clients were, and she felt her job was secure. She loved working with others and being helpful.

Both Sandy's father and mother were white with some Indian heritage. Sandy had grown up in a small town in the Midwest and had married a military man. She had lived through the Gulf War as a young military bride and had birthed a baby, whom she had raised alone until her husband returned to America when the baby was 11 months old. The baby, Cora, was now 14 years of age, and a son, Brad, was 12. Sandy was now divorced, and she and her ex-husband were jointly raising the children. He retained alternating weekend visitation and shared in the major health and education decisions for the children. Sandy's life was busy and hectic, as Cora was involved with varsity volleyball and a part-time weekend job at the local pharmacy, while Brad was active in sports and Boy Scouts, working on one merit badge after another with the goal of becoming an Eagle Scout.

Not only was she busy with the children and her job, but Sandy had managed to carve out time to become active with a biking group and regularly took thirty- to forty-mile road trips on weekends. She loved the feel of a light breeze on her face and the slight soreness and strain of her leg muscles as she cycled along a country road, listening to cows mooing and birds singing and the tires humming, flying along on the asphalt. She felt privileged when she was on the road with her friends or by herself. She rode ten to twelve miles each day.

In addition, Sandy attended to her spiritual needs. She was active in her local church as a Sunday school teacher in her age group. She had grown up in a Southern Baptist church, but she had always felt that the denomination was too rigid. She did still hold to some of the doctrines, but overall she thought that the

Baptists were often hypocritical, smoking and drinking and pretending they didn't. As an adult, she identi-fied as a Presbyterian and had had her children baptized when they were infants.

Sandy couldn't focus on what her client, Julie, was saying, thinking instead about what she knew about lesbians. Lesbians were not totally foreign to Sandy; there had been some in her MSW program. They were—well, they were angry women, women who hung in groups and were intimidating. They were nice enough to her, though, and she was on friendly terms with several of them. But, Sandy thought, Julie wasn't like any of the MSW students that she had encountered.

Sandy was beginning to realize that there were things about this population that she did not understand. Frankly, she was getting uncomfortable with herself. She tried to remember what she had learned about lesbians and identity development. In her MSW program, she had taken a human sexuality class, which had included very open discussion regarding all types of sexuality. But all she really remembered taking away from the class was a feeling that some people were heterosexual and some weren't; she never really thought she would work with any gay or lesbian people.

THE CLIENT

Now as she made herself come back to reality, Sandy listened as Julie talked. Sandy thought to herself, "How could Julie be a lesbian?" Julie Rogers, a Korean American, had first come to the center a year ago for help in adjusting to a return to work when her child, Mary Beth, turned three years old and entered a Montessori day care situation. Julie had worked through those issues and gone on about her life—until today, when she returned to see Sandy. Julie's husband was a successful young African American banker, and Julie was working as an attorney for a local firm that did mostly family law. This young couple had a bright future. Sandy thought that maybe Julie was a little confused. Maybe her husband wasn't as attentive as he should be. Maybe it was just a sexual issue between Julie and her husband. Besides that, Koreans just did not accept homosexuality in their culture.

She willed herself to listen. As Julie continued to talk, Sandy realized that Julie was talking about another female attorney, Anna Taylor. It seemed she and Anna were "attracted" to one another. Julie explained that she and Anna had recently been out of town at a conference and had slept together. Since then, they were inseparable at work and were having a difficult time not touching each other in public. They wanted to spend time alone. Sandy fought to keep out of her mind the images of two women together in a bed, naked.

Julie related that Anna loved little Mary Beth. Sandy gulped and thought, "She's had the baby around that woman." Sandy wondered briefly how this relationship between Julie and Anna might affect Mary Beth's de-velopment and identity. Then Julie began to talk about her husband, Alan, who she said was becoming more and more demanding of her sexually. It was as though he sensed her pulling away and feared losing her. He had even suggested they attend marital counseling. Julie asked Sandy, "What do you think I should do?"

Sandy had a lot of thoughts about what she should do, but she couldn't seem to separate her personal views from the professional ones. She turned the question back to Julie, asking, "What do you want to do?" Julie wasn't sure, but she did want to make another appointment to talk about these issues. Sandy agreed to one more appointment to sort out what the issues were and then discuss any further therapy.

As they scheduled the appointment, Sandy reflected on her ethical responsibilities to Julie. Did she have the appropriate level of competence and comfort to deal with this issue? And if she didn't, what did that say about her skills as a social worker? And what did it say about her ongoing professional relationship with Julie? Despite her misgivings, they set an appointment for the following week.

As Julie walked out the door, Sandy shut it, crossed the room, and collapsed in her chair. She put her head in her hands and sighed heavily, wondering, "What now?" She knew she was in trouble.

CORRESPONDING TEXTBOOK CHAPTERS

Chapter 4: Gay, lesbian, and bisexual identity development, by D. F. Morrow.
Chapter 20: Toward affirmative practice, by L. Messinger.

ADDITIONAL READINGS

Chung, Y. B., & Katayama, M. (1999). Ethnic and sexual identity development of Asian American lesbian and gay adolescents. In K. S. Ng (Ed.), *Counseling Asian families from a systems perspective* (pp. 159–169). Alexandria, VA: American Counseling Association.

Herek, G. M. (1998). Heterosexuals' attitude toward lesbians and gay men: Correlates and gender differences. *Journal of Sex Research, 25*(4), 451–477.

Herek, G. M., & Capitanio, J. P. (1995). "Some of my best friends": Intergroup contact, concealable stigma, and heterosexuals' attitude toward gay men and lesbians. *Personality and Social Psychology Bulletin, 22*(4), 412–424.

Hidalgo, H. (Ed.). (1995). *Lesbians of color: Social and human services.* New York: Haworth.

Laythe, B., Finkel, D., Bingle, R., & Kirkpatrick, L. (2002). Religious fundamentalism as a predictor of prejudice: A two-component model. *Journal of Scientific Study of Religion, 41*(4), 623–636.

National Association of Social Workers. (2000–2003). Lesbian, gay, and bisexual issues. In National Association of Social Workers, *Policy statements* (pp. 193–204). Washington, DC: Author.

———. (1996). *NASW Code of Ethics.* Washington, DC: Author.

Patterson, C. J. (1992). Children of lesbian and gay parents. *Child Development, 6*(3), 1025–1042.

Peplau, L. A., & Amaro, H. (1982). Understanding lesbian relationship. In W. Paul, J. D. Weinrich, J. C. Gonsiorek, & M. E. Hotvedt (Eds.), *Homosexuality: Social, psychological, and biological issues* (pp. 233–247). Beverly Hills, CA: Sage.

QUESTIONS FOR DISCUSSION

1. What are the different concerns (including cultural) of this case study that are important for social workers to understand and to be able to show competence in when working with clients who present similar issues?

2. Sandy is worried about the effect of the lesbian couple on Julie's daughter. What are the known effects on children of being raised in gay and lesbian households?

3. Define and discuss homophobia as it pertains to the case study.

4. Read the *NASW Code of Ethics* for social workers and the NASW Policy Statements regarding homosexuality. Document all/any ethics and/or policies that pertain to the practice of social work in the case study of Sandy Miller.

5. What should Sandy Miller do now that the client is gone and she realizes she is in trouble?

EXERCISE

Name: Facing Our Own Issues

Purpose: To increase social work students' understanding of self so they can work more effectively with GLBT clients. To help students examine their personal feelings, attitudes, beliefs, and ideas about sexual orientation and the sexuality of their clients. To examine social work values and ethics as they affect the client-worker relationship with regard to competence, dignity and work, decision-making skills, and issues of discrimination. To help students learn more about issues related to GLBT clients.

Structure: The activities to be used with this case study are an Inner and Outer Circle exercise. The students will participate in the class discussion, the Inner and Outer Circle, and a debriefing exercise.

Implementation: When class begins, the instructor will hand out pre-test questions. Students will be given 5 minutes to complete the questions and then hand in their responses.

1. What are your feelings and/or thoughts about homosexuality?

2. When did you first learn about this type of sexual orientation?

3. What religion are you and do you practice this religion?

The instructor will talk briefly about the case study discussion and hand out any printed rules for discussion or verbally set rules for the discussion.

After the case study class discussion, the instructor will introduce the Inner and Outer Circle exercise. Students will arrange chairs in two concentric circles. All students will participate as either a role-play participant (seated in the inner circle) or an observer (seated in the outer circle). Roles to be assigned are (1) a gay man who is coming out, (2) a lesbian whose relationship is breaking up, (3) a bisexual person who is trying to find a new partner, (4) a heterosexual person who has recently become aware that his/her teenager has come out as gay, and (5) a transsexual person who has recently lost a friend to AIDS. Those who are playing these roles will constitute the inner circle and will begin to discuss how their issues are affecting them, both positively and negatively.

The students in the outer circle may not speak; they may only listen to the students in the inner circle. The inner circle students talk for approximately 10–15 minutes. Then they move to become the outer circle, and the outer circle becomes the inner circle. The new inner circle members will discuss how it felt to hear the role players and what they thought and felt about the inner circle discussion. They will spend 10–15 minutes discussing how the role players' comments affected them. Then the switch back to the role players occurs and those students discuss what it was like to be part of the role-play and what they understood the observers to say. This last part will take approximately 10–15 minutes.

The following post-test questions should be administered after the case discussion and the class exercise:

1. What was this exercise like for you?
2. What did you learn from this exercise regarding the GLBT population?
3. What did you learn from this exercise about your attitudes?

Debriefing will occur after the post-test is completed, as well as a short discussion addressing the issues brought up in the post-test questions.

Suggested Social Work Courses: Social work practice; HBSE; diversity courses

Suggested Class Size: From 5 to 30 students or more

Materials and Time: Equipment needed is a chalkboard, chalk, desks or table and chairs for students and instructor. This exercise is designed to last one hour.

9

RONALD JACKSON: A MAN ON THE "DOWN LOW"

Robert H. Keefe and Patricia M. Hayes

RONALD JACKSON is a 28-year-old African American male who has come to the community health center following discharge from the state psychiatric facility. Ronald states that he is seeking services at this time for help with medical and mental health care subsequent to being diagnosed with HIV and being left by Tonya, his wife of five years. Ronald also reports that he has recently been diagnosed with depression, which resulted from being fired from his job and separated from his wife and their two-year-old daughter, Ebony, who lives with Tonya.

Ronald claims that he lost his job as a carpenter three years ago when the company for which he had worked for ten years went bankrupt. Ronald states that although Tonya was initially sympathetic, she became increasingly annoyed with him because he did not immediately seek employment but "sat around the house doing nothing all day." Ronald verifies this point, stating that he had "only had enough energy to sit in bed and watch television." He states that he neglected his personal hygiene, brooded over his lost job and what the loss of income would mean for him and his wife, stopped eating meals, and became a "slug."

Ronald states that he and Tonya separated one year ago. He acknowledges that the separation is a major reason for his depression and that he would like to have Tonya back in his life again. When asked about external supports, Ronald states that he used to be active in the local African American Baptist Church, that he coached Little League baseball, and that he helped to develop a neighborhood watch program on the block where he and Tonya lived. He has not participated in any of these activities in months, other than sporadically attending church.

When asked about his HIV diagnosis, Ronald states that he was stunned to find out that he had the "gay disease," insisting that "there is no way in hell" that he's gay, injects drugs, or is a member of a high-risk group. When asked about how he would have contracted the virus, Ronald acknowledges that he lives on the "down low," occasionally secretly having sex with other men. Yet he maintains that his sexual activity with other men doesn't mean he is gay. He states further that although he and his sex partners do not use condoms regularly and he penetrates other men anally, he thought he was safe because he never allows anyone to penetrate him. Besides, he says, "only gays do that." When told that anal penetration without a condom is a high-risk activity for both parties—regardless of who penetrates whom, Ronald reports that he thought the risk was only for the person being penetrated.

During his first session with the agency social worker, Ronald reports that he goes to a gay bar known as the Bottoms Up, located in a neighboring city. He states that he knows some of the men who go there, but he does not have an ongoing relationship with any of them. He states that he has other friends, but he will not go into any detail concerning the nature of these friendships. After further discussion, it appears that Ronald meets these men at the Bottoms Up or at a city park where he and other men go to "hook up." Ronald states he knows Tonya would never have approved of this activity, so he never informed her truthfully about his whereabouts when he would go to the park or the bar. Instead, he would tell her that he was working late on a carpentry project or was seeking freelance work to earn more money.

Upon further discussion, Ronald admits that he goes to a gay bathhouse in a nearby city that caters to African American and Latino men. Ronald reports that there is another bathhouse in the city, but he and other African American men refuse to go to it because it caters primarily to white men. Ronald states there are also "Blatino" parties, "sex parties for black and Latino guys," that he attends on occasion. He will not go into further detail, stating, "The brothers don't want the word to get out to other people."

Ronald states that he has no intention of becoming involved in the gay community because he knows that "I am not gay" and sees no reason to have ongoing relationships with gay men other than to have sex with them. He explains, "Men have to have sex sometimes, and when there are no ladies around, men just know how to help each other out." He states that if any social worker tries to link him to the GLBT community, he will discontinue seeking services, including services that monitor his medication and CD-4 and T-cell counts.

When asked about the important people in his life, Ronald states that although his family of origin lives in the same city as he does, he rarely has any contact with them except for his sister, Miranda. His other two siblings, Clarence and Reginald, are not involved in his life. He reports that Clarence and Reginald think "I'm a faggot and don't want me to come around no more." Ronald's mother died of heart disease two years ago. He has limited contact with his father, whom he believes to have a history of depression that has likely never been treated. He is uncertain about whether his father has been prescribed any medication for the depression.

Since losing his job, Ronald has stopped having contact with his former coworkers. He has also lost contact with the parents of his Little League players, since he is concerned that if people find out that he has HIV, he may not be allowed to continue coaching. Moreover, he is convinced that the pastor and parishioners at the African American Baptist church will think negatively of him if they find out that he has HIV or that he has a history of having sex with other men. He believes that the negative attitude he feels the church has about gay men, divorce, and being unemployed will make them less compassionate about what he is experiencing. As a result, he is reluctant to turn to them for help.

Ronald states, "I don't know what I should expect to get out of going to a social worker since I don't need food stamps. I know I'm not going to no gay support group, so don't even try. But I don't have anyone else who can help."

CORRESPONDING TEXTBOOK CHAPTERS

Chapter 9: Gay male relationships and families, by R. E. McKinney.
Chapter 11: Bisexual relationships and families, by D. L. McClellan.
Chapter 14: Health concerns for lesbians, gay men, and bisexuals, by C. Ryan & E. Gruskin.

ADDITIONAL READINGS

Catania, J.A., Osmond, D., & Stall, R.D. (2001). The continuing HIV epidemic among men who have sex with men. *American Journal of Public Health*, 91(6), 907–914.

Crawford, I., Allison, K. W., & Zamboni, B. D. (2002). The influence of dual-identity development on the psychosocial functioning of African American gay and bisexual men. *Journal of Sex Research*, 39(3), 179–189.

Fullilove, M. T., & Fullilove, R. E. (1999). Stigma as an obstacle to AIDS action: The case of the African American community. *American Behavioral Scientist*, 42(7), 1117–1129.

Lewis, G. B. (2003). Black-white differences in attitudes toward homosexuality and gay rights. *Public Opinion Quarterly*, 67(1), 59–78.

Myers, H. F., Javanbakht, M., Martinez, M., & Obediah, S. (2003). Psychosocial predictors of risky sexual behaviors in African American men: Implications for prevention. *AIDS Education and Prevention*, 15(1, Supplement A), 66–79.

Myrick, R. (1999). In the life: Culture-specific HIV communication programs designed for African American men who have sex with men. *Journal of Sex Research*, 36(2), 159–170.

Wilson, B. D. M., & Miller, R. L. (2002). Strategies for managing heterosexism used among African American and bisexual men. *Journal of Black Psychology*, 28(4), 371–391.

QUESTIONS FOR DISCUSSION

1. Ronald has recently sustained several losses. Considering that he does not think of himself as gay and does not want to submerge himself in the gay community, how would you help him to develop a healthy ecosystem?

2. Consider the theoretical constructs of "sexual orientation," "sexual identity," and "sexual behavior." How are they different from each other, how do they overlap, and how would you help Ronald as a self-identified straight male to come to terms with his same-sex sexual behavior?

3. In general, how would coming from different race, class, and ethnic backgrounds affect sexual identity?

4. Ronald has a psychiatric diagnosis of major depression, and although he engages in sexual encounters with gay men, he refuses to deal with issues having to do with his sexual identity. Discuss how you would go about helping him relieve his depression in light of this fact.

5. Consider your own background. What qualities do you see in yourself that would help you to develop a relationship with Ronald?

6. Ronald reports that he wants his wife back in his life. Discuss the key treatment issues that would need to be addressed if you were to work with them in couples' therapy.

7. The "down low" phenomenon is new to social work literature but not new to the African American community. Because there is little research being done on how to intervene effectively with African American men on the down low, what are some of the things you would do to learn more about this phenomenon so that you could develop your skills more thoroughly?

EXERCISE

Name: Serving Clients Who Are on the "Down Low"

Purpose: To provide students with the opportunity to critically examine the services needed by a client such as Mr. Jackson and how social work values might be operationalized in this instance

Structure: This is a group assignment in which classes are divided into small groups of five to formulate answers to a list of questions. Each question should take the students between 8 and 10 minutes to complete.

Implementation: Instructors will divide their classes into groups of five students each. Each group will be given a copy of questions for consideration (see below). A volunteer from each group will take notes summarizing the group members' responses to each question. The students should take about 8 to 10 minutes per question to discuss their thoughts (40–50 minutes total). The group will select one person to read its responses (preferably not the same student who acted as the transcriber), while the instructor summarizes the points on a chalkboard or marker board (15 minutes).

Suggested Social Work Courses: Generalist practice courses, particularly those at the micro level; courses on HIV/AIDS; courses on working with families.

Suggested Class Size: Fewer than 25 students, in order to ensure the best opportunity for the class to discuss each group's responses. More than five groups would take more time than the instructor would likely want to devote to the assignment.

Materials and Time: Students will need to have pens and paper to write their responses. The instructor will need a chalkboard or whiteboard to summarize the responses from each group. The instructor will also need to have copies of the NASW *Code of Ethics* available for his/her and the students' reference. The exercise should take 75 minutes.

EXERCISE QUESTIONS

As the social worker at the community health center, you will have the responsibility of assisting Mr. Jackson in accessing and coordinating the services he will need for his physical health care, especially as it relates to his HIV status, his mental health, and employment. Given the information in the case study, please answer the following questions:

1. Inasmuch as you are in the first phase of working with Mr. Jackson (exploring/assessing), draw an eco-map to evaluate Mr. Jackson's support systems. Where are the challenges/gaps? Where are the strengths?

Which issue would you help Mr. Jackson to address first? Why? With what areas/people/resources would you begin the process of connecting Mr. Jackson and why?

2. This case involves many ethical issues How would you discuss with Mr. Jackson the prospect of disclosing to his current and past sexual partners, including his wife, his HIV status? What are the legal obligations you must fulfill in your state regarding partner notification? If Mr. Jackson decides that his sexual partners should know that they might have been exposed to HIV, what support/options can you provide for him? If he chooses not to tell them, what will be your course of action and why? As you consider these questions, identify other ethical issues that you believe must be addressed.

3. Although Mr. Jackson has sex with men, he does not consider himself to be gay. What approach would you take with him in talking about safer sex and HIV transmission?

4. In working with Mr. Jackson, how would you operationalize each of the values and ethical issues you identified?

5. It is quite possible that there are few services that are sensitive to the needs of African American men on the "down low." How would you begin to work with your agency to increase your fellow social workers' knowledge base on working with this population?

10

THELMA WITHOUT LOUISE: THE STORY OF AN AGING WOMAN WHO IDENTIFIES WITH WOMEN

Elise M. Fullmer

SADIE, AGE 35, met her neighbor Thelma, age 70, when she moved into the house next door. Sadie had just accepted a job teaching art history at a local private college. She had grown up with a strong grandmother in her own life and had come to appreciate elderly women. As a result, Sadie found herself spending time with Thelma, asking her about her life, and sharing her own daily trials.

Thelma lives in a modest house that she owns, left to her by her father, now deceased. She has lived there for almost twenty years, since she moved home to tend to her father when he became ill. Before she retired to move into her family home, Thelma was for many years a teacher at a small college in the southern part of Oregon.

Now she has some physical problems. She spends much of her time tending her roses, playing with her dogs, talking with the neighbors, and enjoying her sister's family, which includes her nieces and nephews. To them, she is a maiden aunt, the "spinster" sister-in-law. She is an ardent basketball fan and has season tickets to the home games of the local team. For most of the people living around her, however, she is just simply Thelma, one of the older women living in the neighborhood. People don't really distinguish between her and the widows who lived in other nearby houses.

Sadie and Thelma enjoy their talks together and have developed a level of trust and sharing. Sadie has always been open and honest with Thelma about her identity as a lesbian, discussing her relationships and those of her friends. Thelma has seemed comfortable with her and, bit by bit, Sadie has begun to realize that while Thelma would not label herself a lesbian, she has lived a life that paralleled that existence.

When Thelma recalled her youth, she told Sadie about the time she spent in women's bars when she was a young adult and the motorcycle that she drove long before it was acceptable for women to do so. Before moving in with her father, Thelma lived with and raised a child with another woman for fourteen years. Yet she was no longer in touch with this woman. Thelma talked with Sadie about the emotional trauma she experienced when the woman she was living with moved out.

It became clear to Sadie that Thelma was "a sister," but Thelma could not, did not, ever make that connection explicit. She once said to Sadie, "People now are awfully open about their lives and such and that's never been appealing to me. I mean, who cares? What you don't talk about can't hurt you."

CORRESPONDING TEXTBOOK CHAPTERS

Chapter 2: A historical perspective, by L. Messinger.
Chapter 4: Gay, lesbian, and bisexual identity development, by D. F. Morrow.
Chapter 6: Coming out as gay, lesbian, bisexual, and transgender, by D. F. Morrow.
Chapter 13: Gay, lesbian, bisexual, and transgender older people, by E. M. Fullmer.

ADDITIONAL READINGS

Adelman, M. (1986). *Long time passing: Lives of older lesbians*. London: Alyson.

Bozett, F. W. (1989). *Homosexuality and the family*. New York: Harrington Park Press.

Faderman, L. (1991). *Odd girls and twilight lovers: A history of lesbian life in twentieth-century America*. New York: Penguin.

Weston, K. (1991). *Families we choose: Lesbians, gays, kinship*. New York: Columbia University Press.

QUESTIONS FOR DISCUSSION

1. Thelma's biological family saw her as a spinster, and Sadie thought she was a lesbian. How do you think Thelma thought of herself?

2. What influence do affirming or disconfirming models of behavior have on individual identity and development?

3. How might the process of coming out in the later stages of life affect the developmental process?

4. How do stereotypes about being old and being a lesbian interact with each other to create public and private perceptions of self-identity?

5. If Thelma came to see you to talk about coping with loneliness, would you discuss her sexual orientation with her? If so, how? If not, why not?

EXERCISE

Name: Visions of Age and Sexuality

Purpose: To begin to understand how our stereotypes influence the ways in which we categorize and think about people

Structure: Students review pictures of older women and reflect on their assumptions about each one and how they relate to assumptions about aging women and lesbians.

Implementation: The class should do this exercise before reading the case example and before discussion about older lesbians. Students will be asked to look at pictures of older women, one at a time, and jot down words that describe inferences that the students make about the following aspects of their character:

- How old is this woman?
- What was her occupation before reaching old age?
- Does this woman have children or grandchildren?
- This woman was in a relationship for a very long time. Describe the kind of person she was in a relationship with.
- What does this woman do for fun?

The students will record their responses to the above questions (10 minutes). After students have finished their character descriptions, the instructor will ask individual students to volunteer to read their answers aloud, as she or he writes these descriptors on the blackboard (10 minutes). Then, the students will discuss the following questions:

1. Is it likely that one of these women could have been a lesbian? Why or why not?
2. When we see older women, what kinds of stereotypes come into play?
3. How can we tell if someone is (or is not) an older lesbian?
4. When we think about lesbian people, what kinds of stereotypes come into play, particularly with regard to sexuality?
5. When we think about older women, what types of stereotypes come into play with regard to sexuality?

The students will focus on the ways in which these stereotypes conflict with one another, and consider implications for social work practice with older women (20–30 minutes).

Suggested Class Size: 30–40

Suggested Social Work Courses: Gerontology; human behavior; the social environment; practice; GLBT issues

Materials and Time: This exercise requires pictures of two or more older women (the older the better) from a public source such as a magazine or book, paper and writing tools, and a blackboard. The exercise takes 40–50 minutes, depending on the length and depth of the discussion.

PART TWO

COUPLES AND FAMILIES

GLBT PEOPLE have to negotiate many different stereotypes. Historically, gay men have been characterized as hypersexual single people with little interest in lasting relationships and raising children. Bisexuals have been viewed as equally hypersexual, unable to commit to partners of either sex. Transgender people have been exoticized, treated as aberrant people living outside the typical family structure. Lesbians are only recently being recognized as mothers, with the advent of the "gay-by" boom of the 1990s, but even that brings with it expectations and assumptions that may be unwarranted for individual clients. The nine chapters in this section will describe many different couple and family systems that are encountering a variety of struggles and barriers, offering students images of GLBT people that can counter these stereotypes.

Culture, religion, race, age, disability, and class differences are issues for the clients in many of the cases. Chapter 11 introduces a blended lesbian family that is negotiating parenting and relationship challenges in the face of class and age differences. The lesbian couple in chapter 12 struggles with the consequences of the traumatic brain injury of one of the partners. Chapter 13 features an interracial lesbian couple who have adopted two children and recently relocated their family to a new state. Though all three are lesbian couples, they look different, they struggle with their own specific challenges, and they need unique social work responses. Students can compare and contrast these three families and see the diversity within a group.

The remaining cases describe families who are facing crises. In chapter 14 a lesbian couple is struggling with the implications of one partner's developing desire to live as a man. The husband in the heterosexually married couple in chapter 15 is recognizing his own same-sex feelings and preparing to discuss them with his wife. The crisis in chapter 16 is of a different nature: the partners in a lesbian relationship have decided to pursue international adoption, but they still have to work through all the attending political and personal issues, especially with regard to their openness with potential adoption agencies. In chapter 17, another lesbian couple, in the wake of an illness, grapples with their religious and cultural differences as they plan for their eventual deaths. Chapter 18 tells the story of a heterosexual family in which the father is experiencing poor health, drug use, and financial troubles—all rooted in shame and denial about his desire to dress as a woman. Finally, chapter 19 describes the crisis that comes after a successful adoption by a gay male couple, caused by both external and internal stressors. Students can use these cases to gain an understanding of the differences between the "presenting problem" and the "underlying problem," investigating the ways in which issues related to gender and sexuality increase the stresses faced by these families. Students can also examine the roles of culture, class, race, ethnicity, and other factors in the experiences of these families.

11

ARE WE A FAMILY NOW? THE CASE OF MORGAN, SHEA, AND ALEX

Cheryl A. Parks and Nancy A. Humphreys

WHEN MORGAN and Shea first met four years ago at a party hosted by a mutual (lesbian) friend, few who knew them could have imagined they would ever become a couple. Morgan was 38 years old at the time, a successful, college-educated medical professional. She owned and still lived in the house that she and her former partner, Lee, had purchased together during their eleven-year relationship. Lee had left Morgan a year earlier "to find herself." Morgan, devastated by the breakup, had thrown herself into her career and had become progressively more isolated from the gay community. She had fallen into a routine of work, home improvement projects, and visits to her family; she had left little room for friends or the possibility of a new relationship. Although she was "out" as a lesbian among a wide circle of other lesbian friends, Morgan remained "closeted" with her family of origin, at work, and in almost every other area of her life. Morgan had realized and accepted that she was gay while still a teenager, but she was unwilling to talk with her family about her lifestyle for fear that they—particularly her mother—would be disappointed. At work, she had seen and heard too much homophobia to feel safe about coming out there. All of that had worked fine for Morgan until Lee left her. She couldn't talk about what had happened with her family or her coworkers and, after the first couple of months following the breakup, she felt that her friends had become tired of hearing about it. It was just easier to be alone and not dwell on what had happened. She agreed to attend the party, at her best friend's insistence, but she was looking forward to just going home. Then Shea arrived. Something about Shea made her stay.

Shea, just 23 at the time, arrived at the party with a very different story. A tech school graduate working as a hairstylist, Shea had recently separated from Sam, her husband of three years and the father of her 5-year-old son, Alex. Although the separation had occurred for many reasons, a major one (which she had revealed only to her closest friend) was Shea's realization that she was gay. She had been involved in a brief relationship with a woman shortly after leaving her husband, but that episode had ended poorly and she was at the party hoping to meet "someone new." Shea was not "out" to her husband or family, but in the six months since the separation, she had come out to a large circle of friends and coworkers.

Soon after that first meeting, Shea invited Morgan for dinner and, within about two weeks, they were "officially" dating. They didn't talk much about their pasts or what they would want in a future relationship. They were just dating, enjoying their time together, and, much to Morgan's surprise, falling in love. Morgan loved Shea's energy, ambition, and attitude toward life; she "took things in stride," laughed a lot, and enjoyed a good time. Shea admired Morgan's success, her stability, and the sense of security she felt in Morgan's presence.

When Shea's landlord nearly doubled her rent (about three months after they had started dating), she and Alex moved into Morgan's house. In retrospect, both decided that they made the decision much too quickly. They told friends and family that it was a temporary arrangement until Shea could find another apartment, but she never looked and they never talked about making a change. At first things went pretty well—they were in love, they shared a network of friends who were happy to see them together, and Morgan began to feel like her house had turned into a home again. Much to her surprise, she was even enjoying having a child to look after. When "temporary" turned into three months and then into six, they enrolled Alex in school and told their families that it was simply practical for them to continue living together, to share expenses and allow Alex access to a better school district than Shea could afford if she and Alex lived alone. Both families "bought the story," so nobody had to deal, yet, with what their relationship really was.

Later in that first year together, tensions began to surface. Shea had divorced Sam, but in the process he had learned that she was gay. He initially threatened to sue for custody and to tell Shea's parents, but then he agreed to do neither if Shea dropped her demands for child support. Because Morgan could afford to support all three of them herself if needed, Shea agreed. But she did not, as Morgan had requested, insist on Sam's agreeing to reduce Alex's visitation with his father. That led to their first major argument. Alex's behavior after visits with his father was getting worse and worse—he would refuse to listen to his mother or Morgan; he would talk back, throw temper tantrums, and generally show more and more defiance. If Morgan attempted to discipline him, Shea would "come to his rescue" and tell Morgan she was being too strict. Alex's visits with his father became more erratic once Sam began dating, and he frequently missed scheduled visits or made last-minute changes. As a result, Alex's misbehaving escalated, and Morgan and Shea argued more—about the visits, about Alex's behavior and discipline, and eventually about their relationship. Shea wanted to go out on weekends, to dance, drink, and "feel young" again; Morgan had "been there, done that" and preferred staying home. Shea said Morgan was "boring"; Morgan thought Shea needed to settle down and deal with Alex's behavior.

Over the next two years, the couple continued to struggle. The early conflicts continued and new ones emerged. Arguments became both more frequent and more predictable—they would disagree and exchange heated words, then one or the other would eventually give in, and they would make up. Neither of them felt that anything was ever really resolved—they would just back off from each other, and the tension would increase until the next time. Yet both remained committed to staying together. They still loved each other, and even though Morgan felt that Shea excluded her from being a parent to Alex, she did love him and didn't want to see his life disrupted again because of her.

INITIAL AGENCY CONTACT

When Shea, Morgan, and Alex arrived for their intake appointment at the local child and family services agency, only Shea wanted to be there, and she was focused on helping Alex. Alex, now age 9 and in third grade, was the identified "problem": he had been suspended from school for fighting and risked being expelled if he did not get counseling or if another fight occurred. Morgan didn't like the idea of seeking assistance. She had a fairly low opinion of the help that counselors and social workers could offer, and she came along only to "qualify" the counseling for coverage under her health insurance plan.

The insurance coverage was important to both Morgan and Shea. A year earlier, Shea had lost her job and, with it, her health insurance. Morgan's employer had domestic partnership benefits, but Morgan was unwilling to disclose their relationship in order to get Shea and Alex covered. Alex's father's insurance covered Alex, but his plan had no mental health benefits. Without child support or income from Shea, Morgan's resources were stretched to the limit, and she didn't know how they could afford yet another weekly expense. Shea hated being financially dependent on Morgan, but when she had first lost her job, Morgan had encouraged her to go to school full-time and still keep Alex in the after-school program so she would have time to study. So far she had 90 credits, and she had only another year to go to get her BA. For her part, Morgan did want Shea to get her degree without having to work at the same time. Between tuition and child care, though, things were tight. Whenever they argued, Morgan couldn't help feeling resentful that she was doing so much to support the family yet getting so little acknowledgment or cooperation in return.

The couple described two topics that had been the source of most of their arguments in the month before that first counseling appointment—Alex's behavior and an invitation that Morgan had received for her (but not for Shea and Alex) to join her family on a winter vacation. Shea felt excluded by Morgan's family and unacknowledged as Morgan's partner, but she blamed it on Morgan, not them. Morgan still had not directly told her family about their relationship, and she believed they didn't know—an idea Shea thought was ridiculous. How could they "not know" after four years?! (When Shea had disclosed to her parents about two years earlier, they said they "already knew," and after her disclosure they always included Morgan in invitations to family events.) Morgan regularly visited her family without Shea and Alex; she enjoyed that time as a reprieve from some of the tensions at home. This trip offered her a chance to reclaim, however briefly, some sense of the personal and financial freedom she had enjoyed "before." Morgan wanted to go. Shea thought Morgan should insist that Shea and Alex be included in the trip, or not go herself; for Shea, Morgan's decision would speak volumes about how committed she was to their family. Morgan felt that was unfair, and so far she had refused to go along with Shea's demand. Morgan thought Shea was being very selective about when she wanted them to be a family—she certainly didn't seem to think they were a family when it came to Alex; she, and Alex, were both very clear that Morgan was not Alex's parent. Even today, she was only there, really, as a "financial resource."

Alex's behavior—at school and at home—was something they could both agree needed attention. They just didn't agree on what kind of attention or from whom. During the previous school year, Alex had been getting into an increasing number of fights with other kids. The school "blamed" it on "a reaction to all of the changes in his life," but Alex had complained that kids were teasing him because his mother was gay. The guidance counselor suggested counseling for Alex, saying to Shea, "Maybe you and that woman whose house you live in could go as well. I think Alex is confused about what her role is in your life and in his." Shea didn't clarify Morgan's "role," and when she told Morgan, Morgan was furious about being called "that woman"—with the implication that Alex's behavior was somehow her fault and with what she heard as "blatant homophobia." At that point Morgan refused to be a part of any counseling. Now, with the suspension for fighting and Alex's increasing defiance at home—especially after what were now more regular visits with his father and in reaction to anything Morgan said to him—Shea insisted. She hoped counseling would help Alex with his anger and maybe help Morgan and her to arrive at some agreement about rules and discipline. Alex remained silent throughout this history. When asked what he would like to add, he replied, "I dunno," and he refused to say anything more.

CORRESPONDING TEXTBOOK CHAPTERS

Chapter 10: Lesbian relationships and families, by C. A. Parks & N. A. Humphreys.

ADDITIONAL READINGS

Berger, R. (2001). Gay stepfamilies: A triple-stigmatized group. In J. M. Lehmann (Ed.), *The gay and lesbian marriage and family reader: Analysis of problems and prospects for the 21st century* (pp. 171–194). Lincoln, NE: Gordian Knot Books.

Bliss, G. K., & Harris, M. B. (1999). Teachers' views of students with gay or lesbian parents. *Journal of Gay, Lesbian, and Bisexual Identity, 4*(2), 149–171.

Erera, P. I., & Fredriksen, K. (1999). Lesbian stepfamilies: A unique family structure. *Families in Society, 80*(3), 263–270.

Hare, J. (1994). Concerns and issues faced by families headed by a lesbian couple. *Families in Society, 75*(1), 27–35.

Laird, J., & Green, R. J. (1996). *Lesbians and gays in couples and families: A handbook for therapists.* San Francisco: Jossey-Bass.

Lynch, J. M., & Murray, K. (2000). For the love of the children: The coming out process for lesbian and gay parents and stepparents. *Journal of Homosexuality, 39*(1), 1–24

QUESTIONS FOR DISCUSSION

1. Shea provided most of the history presented during this intake appointment, with some input from Morgan and none from Alex. Given what you know, what is your opinion about how motivated each family member is to become involved in therapy? Do all three family members need to be included in the counseling? Why or why not?

2. What do you think Shea's "agenda" is in insisting on counseling? What is Morgan's agenda for coming along? What obstacles to engagement will you face with each member of this family? What strategies will you use to further the engagement with Shea without alienating Morgan? How will you engage Morgan and Alex without alienating Shea?

3. After the initial intake appointment, your supervisor instructs you to develop an initial treatment plan that you will discuss with Shea, Morgan, and Alex at their next appointment. What is your assessment of the top three problems that need to be addressed with this family? What might be the goal(s) of your work on each problem? What treatment modality—individual, couple, or family therapy—would be most beneficial? Would you use different modalities for different problems?

4. Shea and Morgan have formed a blended family comparable to a heterosexual stepparent family. List the major family conflicts revealed in this case presentation and discuss how each is or is not related to the couple's identification as lesbian.

5. There is a fifteen-year age difference between Morgan and Shea. From an adult development perspective, what impact might this have on the couple's relationship and the problems they have described?

6. Alex's behavior—his fighting at school and defiance at home—is identified as the presenting problem. In describing their history together, Shea and Morgan do not suggest that their relationship as a lesbian couple has anything to do with Alex's behavior. What is your opinion about this and how would you address it?

7. Alex and Shea cannot be covered by Morgan's health insurance unless Morgan reveals to her employer that she is lesbian and files required documentation to qualify for domestic partnership benefits. This often includes verification of joint checking accounts, shared domicile, etc., for some specified period, such as "at least twelve months." Typically, heterosexuals are allowed coverage for their spouse and stepchildren without furnishing any proof of relationship beyond a marriage certificate. What is your reaction to this difference in treatment? What are the regulations affecting domestic partner benefits in your area? Are there advocacy organizations in your area that are working to extend the rights that are afforded to heterosexual families to same-sex couples and families?

EXERCISE

Name: Assessing Agency Forms

Purpose: To heighten students' sensitivity to the effects of legal status and agency structures and procedures on lesbian families requesting services from agency-based clinical practice settings

Structure: Students will review agency intake forms and amend them to be more sensitive to GLBT clients. Students then role-play intakes with various clients and test the amended forms. Finally, students will discuss the remaining issues in intake, assessment, and agency policies.

Implementation: Two weeks before scheduling this exercise, the instructor will obtain and distribute to students a copy of the intake forms and policy materials that are typically completed by and given to new clients entering one or more local nonprofit counseling agencies. Students will familiarize themselves with the materials in preparation for the in-class exercise. Students will highlight any questions or text in the intake forms and other materials that they believe might be insensitive to or reflect a bias against GLBT individuals, couples, and families. The instructor will remind students that straight clients may also have GLBT parents, siblings, etc. Preparation also will include reading the Morgan and Shea case, reading the Berger article, and familiarizing themselves with the legal status of lesbian domestic partners and lesbian parents in the state.

When students arrive in class, the instructor will ask for volunteers to role-play the lesbian couple and a social worker during the class exercise.

The instructor will begin the exercise by asking students to identify the questions or text that is insensitive or biased and will record all responses in one column on the board. A student volunteer will then conduct a brief (10-minute) intake interview with one of the role-play couples, using the original intake materials. Observers will record questions that generate incomplete, inaccurate, or guarded responses. At the conclusion of the role-play, the entire class will discuss any additions or deletions needed to the listing of biased/insensitive text. For each item remaining on the list, the class will construct alternative wording to obtain or convey the desired information. Another student volunteer will then conduct a brief intake interview with the second role-play couple, this time using the modified text. The large group will then discuss the differences in the two interviews, the adequacy of the new text for GLBT and heterosexual clients, and the potential for implementing a change in materials used within the agencies in which students are currently placed.

Suggested Social Work Courses: Micro foundation practice; advanced direct practice; family policy; family practice; management and administration

Suggested Class Size: While this exercise could be used in large classes, a smaller class of 15–20 would be most manageable.

Materials and Time: The instructor will need to collect agencies' intake packets for distribution two weeks before the exercise. In class, the instructor will need materials to record student input. This exercise can be completed in one class period, lasting approximately 1 hour.

12

THE CASE OF JOAN AND TERRI: IMPLICATIONS OF SOCIETY'S TREATMENT OF SEXUAL ORIENTATION FOR LESBIANS AND GAYS WITH DISABILITIES

Eileen DeHope

JOAN AND TERRI

In 1993 Joan was a 40-year-old Caucasian woman who had been in a committed relationship for the past seventeen years with a woman named Terri. They lived with their two cats in an old house that they had painstakingly restored. Joan was a news producer at a local TV station where Terri worked as a news reporter. At work, neither of them told her colleagues directly that she was gay or that they were together. However, employees of the TV station enjoyed many parties and gatherings at Joan and Terri's house. Joan and Terri also spent time with many friends who lived close by. They often saw friends weekly for dinner and had an annual week at the beach with those who were closest to them.

Although both Joan and Terri reported having a good relationship, at times Joan's intensity toward work caused a strain between them. In the past, Joan had acknowledged being very focused on her career, and she spent an average of sixty hours a week at work. Terri supported her, but she consistently told Joan that she would like them to spend more leisure time together. Joan stated that she was trying to make a better life for them and as soon as she progressed in her career, she would take more time for herself and their relationship.

THE ACCIDENT

Joan and Terri's life together changed drastically on a vacation trip to Yosemite National Park. While rock climbing, Joan slipped and fell forty feet down the cliff. By applying first aid, Terri was able to save Joan's life. Some nearby hikers heard Terri's anguished screams and went for help. Joan was airlifted to a hospital, where she was diagnosed with a severe traumatic brain injury. As a result of the fall, Joan's skull was opened and her frontal lobe (the area of the brain behind the forehead) was torn. The trauma of her head hitting rock caused further damage to other parts of her brain.

At the hospital, medical staff informed Terri that they could not discuss Joan's case with her as she was not directly related to Joan. Terri explained that they were in a relationship, but the hospital staff stated that they followed "rules" and since Joan and Terri were not married or related by blood, they could not speak to Terri. As a result, Terri could not even visit Joan after she was moved from the emergency room to the intensive care unit—unless Joan's family consented. Terri contacted Joan's parents to let them know of the accident. Upon their arrival at the hospital, the parents further restricted Terri's visitation and involvement with Joan. At a family meeting with the social worker at the hospital, Joan's family stated that Terri was "just a roommate" and not significant to Joan.

Upon being ostracized by the hospital and Joan's family, Terri hired a lawyer to see if she could at least gain visitation rights. She really wanted to have full decision-making rights for Joan; she had a medical power of attorney that Joan had signed stating as much. A judge denied both hospital visitation and Terri's right to be Joan's surrogate decision maker, ruling that Joan and Terri's relationship was neither legal nor sanctioned by society, thereby nullifying any contracts between them. As a result, Joan's parents were deemed full guardians of their daughter.

As Joan came slowly out of a coma, Joan's parents transferred her to a traumatic brain injury rehabilitation program that was five hundred miles away from Terri. Clinically, Joan presented with little memory or awareness. She could not walk, speak, or feed herself. At the rehabilitation program, Joan's parents forbade Terri from coming to see Joan, stating that Terri upset their daughter. Further, Joan's family began to dismantle her monetary assets, including freezing Joan and Terri's joint checking account and selling her half of the house that they lived in. Terri moved with the cats to a one-bedroom apartment after the house was sold. Because work provided too many memories of Joan, Terri left her job and obtained employment at a competing TV station.

Over time, Joan began to regain some functioning, moving from a wheelchair to a walker to use of a cane for mobility. She learned how to feed and bathe herself and put her clothes on. She began to speak again but still lacked any self-awareness. She was very confused and often could not understand simple directions. She did not remember her parents, Terri, or anything about her life. When confused, she yelled at other people.

TEN YEARS LATER

After ten years, Joan progressed to living in a community-based neuro-rehabilitation group home with other people who had similar injuries. Joan's behavior became more controlled, but her memory continued to be poor. She often would ask others why she was not married or why she had no children. When staff provided her the information that she had lived with a woman for seventeen years, Joan appeared to be confused. She often replied that her father had told her that she was committed to her career and did not have time for a family.

Finally this year, clinical staff of the group home arranged for Terri to visit Joan without her father's knowledge. The staff felt it was important for the two women to connect, since Joan often was confused by the past she could not remember. The meeting was strained, as Terri realized that Joan did not remember anything about her or their relationship. Joan was polite but appeared very confused by Terri's information, as it was inconsistent with what Joan's father had told her about her past. Terri has not directly contacted Joan since their meeting. She has, however, sent Joan cards and flowers for special occasions.

CORRESPONDING TEXTBOOK CHAPTERS

Chapter 3: Oppression, prejudice, and discrimination, by D. E. Elze.
Chapter 10: Lesbian relationships and families, by C. A. Parks & N. A. Humphreys.
Chapter 14: Health concerns for lesbians, gay men, and bisexuals, by C. Ryan & E. Gruskin.

ADDITIONAL READINGS

Baker, K., Tandy, C., & Dixon, D. (2002). Traumatic brain injury: A social worker primer with implications for practice. *Journal of Social Work in Disability and Rehabilitation, 1*(4), 25–44.
National Trust. http://www.nationaltrust.org.in/guardian_ship.htm.
Thurman, D. (2001). The epidemiology and economics of head trauma. In L. Miller & R. Hayes (Eds.), *Head trauma: Basic, preclinical, and clinical directions* (pp. 327–347). New York: Wiley.

QUESTIONS FOR DISCUSSION

1. Describe the social policies that affected Joan and Terri's relationship over the past ten years. Has anything changed? What legal rights do gay couples have today in cases like Joan and Terri's? If you do not know, how would you find information on the rights of gay couples?

2. How does this case reflect theories of human development, particularly development of sexuality? What do you think about Joan's inability to remember her own sexuality after a traumatic brain injury?

3. What is self-awareness? How does it affect self-growth? How does memory affect self-awareness and self-growth?

4. If you were a social worker in the hospital where Joan was taken, what would you have done to help Joan, her family, and Terri?

5. If you were a social worker in the group home where Joan resides, how would you have handled the meeting between Joan and Terri?

6. What do you know about traumatic brain injury? How would you find out information if you were working with a client who had such an injury?

7. How and why do hospitals make policies that do not recognize GLBT families? How might a social worker address this?

8. How could a social worker advocate for Terri's rights as Joan's partner?

EXERCISE

Name: Challenges in Case Management

Purpose: To allow the student to understand the practice implications of society's treatment of lesbians and gays when they experience a disability

Structure: In small groups, students will review the case scenario and imagine themselves to be Joan's case manager at the community-based neuro-rehabilitation center. As such, they will consider questions and report their decisions.

Implementation: Students will read the case study before coming to class. When they arrive in class, they will be separated into groups of three and asked to imagine the following scenario and answer these questions (which should be written on the board or displayed on an overhead projector):

You are a social worker at a community-based neuro-rehabilitation center. You are Joan's case manager. Would you assist Joan with establishing a relationship with Terri? Why or why not? Identify the issues that would arise regarding guardianship, confidentiality, family systems, sexual identity.

The team of three students will appoint someone to take notes of their discussion about how they, as a case manager for Joan, would handle the situation with Terri (10 minutes). Their summary will then be presented to the larger class for further discussion (15 minutes).

Suggested Social Work Courses: Practice and field classes

Suggested Class Size: 30 maximum

Materials and Time: A blackboard or a whiteboard, materials for taking notes, and (possibly) an overhead projector and transparency. The exercise will take about 25 minutes.

13

A FAMILY IN TRANSITION

Cathryne L. Schmitz and Janet Wright

BETSY HAS been a school social worker in an urban school in the upper Midwest for the past five years. The city and the school have changed rapidly over the past decade, with increasing diversity and shifting social systems. Betsy is aware of the need for taking a proactive approach in educating the school community of teachers, students, and staff about the impact of these changes. She is presently working with a child who has motivated her to take leadership in beginning the process.

REFERRAL

Several weeks ago, a 6-year-old boy, Joseph, was referred to Betsy by his teacher. Joseph is new to the school this year, and although his grades are adequate, he does not seem to be adjusting. He is socially isolated and inattentive in class. The teacher says that recently he seems anxious and is exhibiting some disruptive behavior. When reviewing his former school records, Betsy sees that he has not previously had academic or behavioral problems.

When Betsy met with Joseph, he reported that the other children didn't like him and he wanted to go back to his old school and his old home. He also said that he didn't like being at school and away from his sister, *abuela*, and parents, whom he called Mama and Mommy. After meeting with Joseph, Betsy called his mothers, Rosa and Karen. His parents also were concerned and eager to meet with Betsy. They recognized that the move had been difficult for all of them socially, even though it was professionally a good change. A meeting was scheduled in two days at Betsy's office.

INTAKE AND ASSESSMENT

During the initial meeting, Joseph's parents explained that the family had moved from Seattle, Washington, to their new home this past summer when Rosa accepted a tenure track position as a mathematics professor at one of the public universities. Karen is a nurse and she took a job in the local hospital. Carmen, Rosa's 80-year-old mother, also moved in with them in their new location. The children like having their *abuela* in the house, but the lack of privacy is requiring some adjustment for Rosa and Karen. Carmen is helpful with the children, but her health is fragile. She has diabetes and heart disease, which is also a stressor for the family.

Karen and Rosa reported that they are all experiencing the loss of friends as well as the loss of a community that was diverse in race, ethnicity, language, and sexual orientation. Joseph and his sister, Maria, are frightened when their parents leave them to go to work. As a result, Rosa and Karen are trying to juggle their schedules so one of them can be with the children most of the time. Carmen fills in when they are both at work. Rosa and Karen, however, have no time together and are increasingly stressed. Maria has been sneaking in to sleep with them at night, leaving them tired. Consequently, they have even less patience with Joseph's acting out at home. Because of all the demands on their energy, Rosa and Karen have not begun to explore their options for establishing community connections in their new city.

Betsy was able to gather substantial information on the family's history during a series of three meetings with them. Rosa and Karen have been together as a couple for twelve years and have been through many changes during that time. When they met, Rosa was 26 years old. She had been involved with her high school sweetheart until the year before she met Karen, who was 24 years old and had never been involved with a woman before. Together, they explored what it meant to be a lesbian. Because of Rosa's concerns about placing shame on her family, they were closeted and secretive during the first six years of their relationship. These dynamics created distance between them and placed a strain on the relationship.

Their commitment to the relationship led them to seek the support of a social worker regarding their concerns about being lesbian and about the self-esteem and communication problems that resulted. It was at that time that Rosa became less secretive with her family and Karen began her involvement with the gay, lesbian, bisexual, and transgender (GLBT) community. Karen has been politically active, working on GLBT issues. Rosa, who is from a Latino family with roots that go back seven generations in New Mexico, has been hesitant to take a public stand.

As their relationship grew stronger and they formed a family, Karen and Rosa wanted children. Two years ago, they were able to adopt Joseph and Maria, who were 4 and 2 years old at the time. Because they lived in Washington State at the time of the adoption, they were able to adopt both children as a couple. They feel that the adoption has been very important for solidifying their family and a source of strength during this transition.

Betsy also found out about the children's history before they were adopted. The children's birth mother, Esmeralda, had moved to Seattle with her mother from El Salvador as an adolescent. She died of cancer when Maria was only 10 months old. After Esmeralda's death, the children stayed with their maternal grandmother for a few months, but her health was not good. Their father, who is biracial, moved out of the state before Maria was born, and no one knows where he is. The children had no other family in the United States. Joseph and Maria lived in two foster homes before placement with Karen and Rosa. Joseph experienced some physical and emotional abuse in one of the homes.

Rosa, Karen, and the children have always lived together in multiracial communities. The children and Rosa are bilingual, while Karen struggles to learn Spanish and is improving. The children have ongoing contact with their birth grandmother and are close to Rosa's family. Rosa's father died when she was 22 years old, but she has a large extended family that is very close. Her brother and cousins know about Rosa and Karen's relationship. The older relatives have not been told, but they include Karen as a family member and never question their relationship. The children also know Karen's parents, but haven't spent much time with them. They live in Arizona in a gated community that does not allow children, so it is uncomfortable to visit.

INTERVENTION

After spending time with the family and hearing their story, the social worker thought she had the information she needed to begin working with the family. Together, Betsy and the parents outlined the following goals and initial action steps:

1. Establish a support system for the family and also for Karen and Rosa's relationship as a couple.

   - Karen will contact the GLBT center this week to find out about possible support groups.
   - Rosa will visit the new local multi-service center, El Centro de Esperanza, to find out about the local Latino/a community and the services and activities at the center for children and families.
   - Rosa will contact people connected with Spanish and Latino/a studies at the university.

2. Set aside a weekly time for Karen and Rosa to be alone together.
   - Rosa will ask Carmen to care for the children on Friday evenings.

3. Find quality health care for Carmen.

   - The social worker will explore possible state/federal health care programs for the elderly.
   - Karen will talk with the finance department at the hospital about different health programs.

4. Develop a support system for Joseph.

- Rosa will explore programs for children at El Centro de Esperanza.
- Karen will ask about family and children's activities at the GLBT center.
- The social worker will (a) include Joseph in a weekly lunch bunch that she has organized to help students who are experiencing transitions, (b) work with Joseph's teacher about positive ways to engage him in learning as well as social activities, (c) see about arranging activities that engage children in learning about diverse cultures, and (d) approach the principal and vice principal about training and curriculum development on issues of diversity and oppression.

Rosa and Karen agreed to meet again with the school social worker in two weeks to determine their next steps. The social worker assured them that they could call her in the meantime if they had questions or concerns.

CORRESPONDING TEXTBOOK CHAPTERS

Chapter 10: Lesbian relationships and families, by C. A. Parks & N. A. Humphreys.

ADDITIONAL READING

Anzaldua, G. (1987). *La frontera/borderlands: The new mestiza*. San Francisco: Spinsters/Aunt Lute.

Hidalgo, H. (1995). The norms of conduct in social service agencies: A threat to the mental health of Puerto Rican lesbians. *Journal of Gay and Lesbian Social Services*, 3(2), 23–41.

Patterson, C. (1996). Lesbian mothers and their children: Findings from the Bay Area Families Study. In J. Laird & R. J. Green (Eds.), *Lesbians and gays in couples and families* (pp. 420–437). San Francisco: Jossey-Bass.

Swigonski, M. E. (1995). The social service needs of lesbians of color. *Journal of Gay and Lesbian Social Services*, 3(2), 67–83.

Wright, J. (2001). Aside from one little, tiny detail, we are so incredibly normal: Perspectives of children in lesbian stepfamilies. In M. Bernstein & R. Reinmann (Eds.), *Queer families, queer politics* (pp. 272–292). New York: Columbia University Press.

QUESTIONS FOR DISCUSSION

1. What are the strengths of Joseph, his parents and family, the school, and the community?

2. What are the strengths of the Latino/a culture and also the GLBT culture/community that may be particularly helpful for this family?

3. What changes does the school need to make to better serve children and families who contribute to the school's diversity through their race/ethnicity and sexual orientation?

4. What additional information would you like to collect? Why?

5. What additional goals or interventions might be helpful?

6. Rosa and Karen are both professionals. How might this situation be different if they had minimum-wage or low-paying jobs?

7. Does your state allow GLBT couples to adopt children? Why or why not?

8. Does your state allow lesbians and gay men to enter into a civil union or marriage? What would be the reasons for not allowing a civil union or marriage? What is the difference between these two?

EXERCISE

Name: In the Name of Love

Purpose: To help students understand the privileges and benefits of same-sex marriage

Structure: Students engage in a brainstorming exercise.

Implementation: Students are asked to meet in small groups of three to five to identify all the ways in which marriage benefits heterosexual partners and their children (10–15 minutes). After the groups have assembled their lists, a representative from each group will report that group's list to the larger class. The instructor will record these on a flipchart or whiteboard (10–15 minutes). Students will then consider which of these benefits are available to same-sex partners and their families, which are unavailable, and what the implications of these differences are for the functioning and health of these couples and their families.

Suggested Social Work Courses: HBSE; family practice; family policy

Suggested Class Size: 20–25

Materials and Time: This exercise requires only a whiteboard or flip chart. It lasts 45–60 minutes.

14

FROM LESBIAN RELATIONSHIP TO TRANS/LESBIAN RELATIONSHIP

Arlene Istar Lev

MOLLY, A 36-YEAR-OLD white woman, and Sid, a 38-year-old Latina, entered therapy in a state of turmoil and distress. Long-term lesbian lovers and the parents of two small children, they saw themselves as "survivors," with well-honed skills in weathering relationship challenges. After nearly twelve years together, they had coped with the rejection of Molly's fundamentalist Christian family and had struggled with five years of frustrating infertility and the successful pregnancy and birth of now 4-year-old twins with the help of expensive and invasive reproductive medicine. Molly said, "I really thought we could coast now, but I honestly don't know if our marriage can survive this."

This crisis in the relationship was initiated by Sid's disclosure that she was no longer comfortable living as a woman. This disclosure came as a shock to Molly, who, although aware of Sid's gender discomfort, had had no idea that Sid would ever consider transitioning to live as a man. Sid had always strongly identified as a "butch." She was very masculine in appearance and chose employment in a traditional male trade. Until this disclosure, Molly had always thought Sid was satisfied in her identity as a lesbian woman; however, Sid now expressed a lifelong unhappiness and discomfort that she felt only sex reassignment would alleviate.

Both Sid and Molly identified as strong feminists and were active in lesbian politics long before they became lovers. Molly felt that Sid's disclosure was an insult to the lives they had lived as out lesbians and saw Sid's desire to transition as a form of "internalized misogyny." She was very clear that she was not interested in being involved in a heterosexual relationship, or even being seen that way publicly.

Sid was mostly silent while Molly expressed her anger, but when she was invited to speak her words were direct and tears were in her eyes. "I love Molly and this family more than anything in the world, but I cannot live like this anymore. I simply do not feel like a woman, and I need to transition and live full-time as a man."

CORRESPONDING TEXTBOOK CHAPTERS

Chapter 5: Transgender identity, by J. I. Martin & D. R. Yonkin.
Chapter 12: Transgender emergence within families, by A. I. Lev.

ADDITIONAL READINGS

Bolus, S. (2000). Transgendered butches and FTMs: A uniquely femme perspective. *Femme: The Magazine*. Retrieved May, 13, 2002, from http://www.stonefemme.com/FemmeMagazine/cover.htm.

Cromwell, J. (1999). *Transmen and FTMs: Identities, bodies, genders, and sexualities*. Champaign: University of Illinois Press.

Devor, H. (1997). More than manly women: How female-to-male transsexuals reject lesbian identities. In. B. Bullough, V. L. Bullough, & J. Elias (Eds.), *Gender blending* (pp. 87–102). Amherst, NY: Prometheus Books.

Green, J. (2001) The art and nature of gender. In F. Haynes & T. McKenna (Eds.), *Unseen genders: Beyond the binaries* (pp. 59–70). New York: Peter Lang.

Halberstam, J. (1998). *Female masculinity*. Durham, NC: Duke University Press.

Hale, C. J. (1998). Consuming the living, dis(re)membering the dead in the butch/FTM borderlands. *Gay and Lesbian Quarterly, 4*(2), 311–348.

Lev, A. I. (1998, October). Invisible gender. *In the Family*, 8–11.

QUESTIONS FOR DISCUSSION

1. What do you see as the salient issues that Molly and Sid have to negotiate in order to remain in a committed relationship?

2. If Sid does transition, is Molly still a lesbian?

3. Whether or not the relationship survives, how should this information be shared with their children?

4. What questions would you ask Sid about his "need" to transition?

5. What are the differences between being a butch lesbian and a transsexual man?

6. Do you think the struggles for Molly reside in a more personal, intimate context (i.e., their sex life) or in the more social and public area (i.e., how this will affect her standing in the lesbian community)?

7. Do you think this marriage can be saved? Do you think it should be saved? If so, what would you do to help them save their marriage?

EXERCISE

Name: Brainstorming Identity

Purpose: To demonstrate the difference between sexual orientation and gender identity and how they overlap

Structure: Students brainstorm definitions about the four parts of sexual identity (sex, gender identity, gender role, and sexual orientation), then apply these to the case study.

Implementation: The instructor will write on the blackboard the following terms, leaving space below each one to fill in attributes:

Sex   Gender Identity   Gender Role   Sexual Orientation

The instructor will then ask students to define the terms and will write their responses on the board (10 minutes). Once students seem to understand these differences, the instructor will ask them to review Molly and Sid's case and describe each partner in this case study according to the four parts of sexual identity (20 minutes).

Suggested Social Work Courses: Social work practice or human behavior courses addressing issues in sexual orientation and gender identity

Suggested Class Size: 15–25

Materials and Time: This exercise requires only a blackboard or flip chart. It should take no more than 30 minutes.

15

ALAN'S STORY: A HETEROSEXUALLY MARRIED COUPLE FACES A SEXUAL IDENTITY CRISIS

David Jenkins

THE FOLLOWING is a journal assignment shared with the therapist:

Mary and I started dating when we were 17 years old. Before this time, we each had some dating experience during our sophomore and junior years of high school. Even though we were attending the same high school, Mary and I knew each other only through mutual friends. Our actual interaction up until our senior year had been quite limited. We started to date after I finally got up the courage to ask her out during our senior year.

Both Mary and I were raised in white, middle-class, Southern Baptist homes. While brought up in the same city, we attended different churches. As part of my upbringing, I was taught that I needed to date and marry only a nice Southern Baptist woman and should not even consider other women. At our high school, there were only two women that I found attractive who fit the Baptist qualification. Since Mary was pretty, popular, and a Southern Baptist, I considered her to be a "good catch."

Mary and I had a wonderful first date and I got up the courage to ask her out again two weeks later. After the second date, I believed I had found a wonderful woman to get to know. We quickly became the best of friends and shared many interests and activities. Mary and I continued to date for the remainder of our senior year and dated exclusively through college. We became engaged during our junior year of college and planned to marry about the time of graduation. We were married just two weeks after my graduation from college. She would finish up her degree a few months after our marriage.

Before my marriage, I recognized I had an attraction to men. However, given my religious background, I considered my attractions as "temptations from the devil" and not really a valid concern to be examined. I was taught that homosexuality was a sin and unacceptable. Furthermore, any sexual orientation beyond heterosexuality didn't even exist in my religion. I had been taught that someone who identified as gay or lesbian was not really gay but was being misled by Satan. So, even with these attractions, I continued to identify as heterosexual. I remember praying that God would take away any temptations or attractions I had toward men. At this point I believed those feelings would go away. I also trusted I was doing the right thing by dating a woman and planning to get married and start a family.

Another aspect of my family set the tone for not accepting homosexuality. My father came out when I was 16, just a few weeks before I began my senior year of high school. My older sister and I had noticed the increasing time he spent away from the family and his intense friendships with different men. I gathered some additional evidence of my concerns and finally confronted my mother with this issue. Later that same day, she went to discuss this with my father. During this conversation, he not only confessed his sexuality but also admitted he was in love with a man.

Although initially denying the truth to my sister and me, my mother and father later acknowledged his sexual orientation. My father attended some therapy to try once again to be heterosexual but soon decided it would not work. He left his marriage to my mother about three months after the initial confrontation. My mother was devastated with the realization of the end of her marriage. I now believe it wasn't the real loss of her husband that caused the strong reaction, but the public humiliation of admitting that her husband was gay and her marriage wasn't perfect. In a way, she wore his sexuality as her own "badge of shame." My father also experienced great loss in his coming out. In addition to his loss of his marriage and his diminished contact with his children, my dad's brother and parents swiftly cut him out of family businesses and interaction. Friends from our Baptist church offered my mother, my sister, and me their support and prayers that my father would see the error of his ways and return to his family. If I hadn't known it before, I was now clear that God did not want me, or anyone, to be homosexual. I remember thinking I would never admit or discuss any of my personal struggles with anyone.

Near the time we were to get married, Mary began to struggle with visible signs of anorexia. She lost a great deal of weight and seemed to be thrilled that she would be skinny for her wedding day. Her family became alarmed at her weight loss and I became involved in the struggle to get her some help. In my naiveté about the seriousness of her illness, I secretly believed I could rescue her and ultimately help her recover from this difficulty. I thought that if she and I got married, she would get away from her family and could start fresh in a healthy environment where we both would flourish. Mary's anorexia, and later bulimia, became a consuming element for the first six years of our marriage.

Even though I do not like to admit this, Mary and I created a strange relationship in the early days of our marriage. I ended up taking much of the responsibility for things, while she obsessed about her weight and food. In the most simplistic terms, she was the "sick one" and I was the "healthy one." When we were not at work or at church, Mary would exercise for hours at a time. She would rise early and go to bed late in an effort to exercise just a bit more before the next day began. During this time, I would obsess over ways to help her get well or ways to hide the severity of her struggle from others. I would read any book or article I could find to help Mary with her disorder. Because Mary often refused to eat in front of others, we became very isolated and did not interact with a lot of other people. I now believe I was ashamed of her struggle and the fact that I couldn't fix her through our relationship.

During this overwhelming struggle in our marriage, I continued to find men attractive. Throughout our first years of marriage, I was active in various sports and had several male friends. I found it strange that I not only enjoyed the sports but also found myself desiring the men that I saw. The anorexia and bulimia left little time and energy to devote to my own issues. I believed we had much more important items than being concerned about my attractions to men. Furthermore, I wasn't going to discuss this with my spouse, who I believed to be in a fragile state of mind.

Mary's eating disorder got to be less of a problem when we moved to another state to pursue furthering our careers. I think moving away from our families and having to become more independent helped our relationship. As things seemed to be improving, Mary and I discussed beginning our family. We both wanted to have children and tried for a few years to conceive, but we had no luck. Mary and I finished up our graduate degrees and moved to a large urban area to work. Since school was complete, we were now ready to have children. Given our inability to conceive in the past, we decided to consult a fertility doctor. With the doctor's assistance, we were able to conceive in about six months. We were pregnant and overwhelmed with joy.

About this same time, my sister announced that she was a lesbian. Even though Mary and I both had had suspicions about this in the past, we loved my sister and didn't give her singleness and possible homosexuality a lot of thought. After this disclosure, I talked at length to my sister about her struggles with and ultimate acceptance of her sexuality. The reality of now having a gay father and a lesbian sister was a challenge, requiring me to rethink my religious beliefs about homosexuality in the face of my love of my family. Mary agreed that it was hard to believe that these people we loved were going to hell. However, I was about to begin a mission. I wanted to find out more on the topic of sexuality and what Scripture really said about it. I wanted to form my own beliefs about this issue. I began to read outside of the limited literature I had found in the Southern Baptist Church. I was amazed to find that there were other interpretations of Scripture beyond what I had been taught. I even found authors who stressed that it was possible to be gay and Christian. This was a radical assault on my previous beliefs.

Slowly, I am beginning to think I am finding some new truths. Could God actually create various sexual orientations? I read these books in front of Mary and discuss with her the things I am learning. Although she listens, she doesn't seem to be really concerned about this issue. I suppose that this is more my journey than hers. Internally, I notice a shift about my reading. No longer do I read just to benefit my beliefs about my father or sister; this is about me. As I continue to read and become knowledgeable, I am now almost convinced that my feelings, my desires, are not evil or from Satan. I am beginning to believe that they could be a basic, God-given orientation. I know I need to face my feelings and discuss this topic with Mary.

CORRESPONDING TEXTBOOK CHAPTERS

Chapter 9: Gay male relationships and families, by R. E. McKinney.
Chapter 11: Bisexual relationships and families, by D. L. McClellan.
Chapter 17: Religion and spirituality, by D. F. Morrow & B. Tyson.

ADDITIONAL READINGS

Buxton, A. (1994). *The other side of the closet: The coming-out crisis for straight spouses and families* (rev. and expanded ed.). New York: John Wiley.
Lowe, B. W. (2002). A letter to Louise: A biblical affirmation of homosexuality. Retrieved September 26, 2004, from http://www.godmademegay.com.
Spong, J. (1988). *Living in sin: A bishop rethinks human sexuality*. New York: HarperCollins.
——. (1991). *Rescuing the Bible from fundamentalism: A bishop rethinks the meaning of scripture*. New York: HarperCollins.
White, M. (1995). *Stranger at the gate: To be gay and Christian in America*. New York: Plume/Penguin.
Whitehead, S. (1997). *The truth shall set you free: A family's passage from fundamentalism to a new understanding of faith, love, and sexual identity*. San Francisco: HarperCollins.

QUESTIONS FOR DISCUSSION

1. Do you believe it was a mistake for Alan and Mary to get married?

2. Is it possible to salvage this marriage? How might this help or harm various members of this family?

3. As a social worker, what services or resources would you recommend to Alan and Mary before Alan discloses his struggle with his sexuality? What would you offer them if Alan comes out?

4. Describe the role that you think religion/spirituality will continue to play in the lives of Alan and Mary after this revelation.

5. Discuss why you agree or disagree that Alan was "the healthy one" in the relationship.

6. What would you suggest Mary and Alan do about the approaching birth of their child?

7. What would you consider to be the "best interest" of the child?

EXERCISE

Name: Sexual Identity Crisis

Purpose: To allow students to experience the emotions, motivations, fears, and intentions of a family where a spouse is going through a sexual identity crisis

Structure: Students will read the case example, identify issues and emotions facing families in which one member is going through a sexual identity crisis, and role-play those issues in a therapy setting.

Implementation: After reading the case example, the instructor will announce that the class will be attempting to develop greater empathy and understanding for having these types of family members as clients. Students will then be placed in one of the three small groups. One group will take the part of the straight spouse in the family. The second group will represent the spouse who is going through the sexual identity crisis. The third group will play the role of the social worker who is working with this couple. Students will brainstorm the concerns and issues of each particular member of the client system, identifying what they believe to be the emotions, motivations, fears, and intentions of their assigned individual (10–15 minutes). They will then break up into groups of three (one from each group) and role-play an interaction (10–15 minutes). After role-playing is complete, the class will reconvene as a whole to discuss the concerns and issues of being each particular member of the client system (30 minutes).

Suggested Social Work Courses: Practice, family practice, or practice with couples; human behavior and the social environment

Suggested Class Size: Up to 25 students. Groups probably need to be limited to allow members the comfort to discuss the concerns and issues of their part of the client system.

Materials and Time: Sufficient space for the three groups, as well as seating for the family-type interviews in groups of three. The exercise will take 45–60 minutes.

16

SEEKING A CHILD THROUGH INTERNATIONAL ADOPTION: LUCY'S AND ROBIN'S STORY

Nancy A. Humphreys and Cheryl A. Parks

LUCY (AGE 35) and Robin (age 39), both white, who have been together for seven years, have been in couples counseling with social worker Ann Foster for several months, working on family and relationship issues. Each has also been seeing an individual clinical social worker. Within the first few months of their work together, many of the relationship issues that had brought them into counseling were addressed. They were feeling more comfortable with one another and, most important, better able to talk through their continuing issues without an outsider.

As their relationship improved, they returned to discussing an issue that was an important part of their beginnings as a couple, specifically an interest in having a child. This has been a particularly strong desire on Lucy's part, and given their newfound comfort with their relationship, Robin (who is more commonly known as Rob) was now also willing to consider becoming a parent. In their joint counseling sessions, Lucy and Rob started discussing in detail the possibilities of becoming parents. After many discussions on their own and a few counseling sessions, they decided to pursue assisted insemination.

What followed was several expensive, frustrating, and ultimately unsuccessful efforts to inseminate Lucy, who not only wanted to parent but also wanted the experience of being pregnant. The excitement of anticipating a positive result and the pain over their lack of success became common subjects during Lucy and Rob's counseling sessions. They expressed their many frustrations in trying to coordinate two busy work schedules so they could both be available during the narrow window of opportunity during which ovulation occurred. These frustrations, along with the expense of repeated inseminations (which was not covered by health insurance), placed new strains on their relationship.

Ultimately Lucy and Rob decided to explore the idea of adoption, especially international adoption, since they both wanted to have an infant. They had heard that most children available for adoption in the United States are older, racially mixed, or physically challenged in some way. They expressed a willingness to parent a more challenging child as a second addition to their family at a later time.

In their joint sessions, Lucy and Rob expressed a significant and shared concern: their confusion about what is and is not possible and permissible, given that they are lesbians. They also disagreed about whether it would be better to adopt as an openly lesbian couple or, instead, to have Lucy adopt without Rob's official involvement.

Both Lucy and Rob, of course, expressed many conflicting feelings during the counseling sessions. Each had strong feelings about her own position. Lucy was willing to adopt alone but strongly preferred that the adoption be open so that both she and Rob could be equal parents. Rob was very conflicted over whether she was ready to be "outed." She also worried that if they once acknowledged the true nature of their relationship, there would be no way of "getting the genie back into the bottle" later if their lesbianism became an impediment to adoption.

As it happened, Ann had a background in working in adoption and therefore had some knowledge, but she was concerned that it was quite dated. In thinking through her approach to working with Lucy and Rob, Ann felt comfortable and confident that she could help them with the emotional struggles. However, she was also aware that the couple would be best served by having the most up-to-date legal and policy information available, specific to international adoptions. Ann remembered hearing something about the Hague Convention, which regulates inter-country adoption of children, and that the issue of sexual orientation is a big factor in this new policy. After making a few telephone calls to local colleagues working in the field of adoption, she learned that a social worker named Carol Halbertson, located in a major urban area not too far from where Lucy and Rob lived, was willing to consult with other social workers or lesbian couples interested in international adoption.

At their next appointment, Ann shared with Lucy and Rob what she had learned and they decided to contact Carol Halbertson directly to get more information about what is and is not possible, given the Hague Convention. Lucy and Rob decided to continue to work with Ann on their relationship and feelings about adoption and all that it will mean.

CORRESPONDING TEXTBOOK CHAPTERS

Chapter 10: Lesbian relationships and families, by C. A. Parks & N. A. Humphreys.
Chapter 19: Social welfare policy and advocacy, by L. Messinger.

ADDITIONAL READINGS

Baetens, P., & Brewaeys, A. (2001). Lesbian couples requesting donor insemination: An update of the knowledge with regard to lesbian mothers. *Human Reproduction Update, 7*(5), 512–519.
Gustausson, N. S. (1995). "Don't ask, don't tell" and child welfare. *Social Work, 40*(6), 815–817.
Hartman, A. (1996). Social policy as a context for lesbian and gay families. In J. Laird & R. J. Green (Eds.), *Lesbian and gays in couples and families: A handbook for therapists* (pp. 69–85). San Francisco: Jossey-Bass.
Hillis, L. (2001). Intercountry adoption under the Hague Convention: Still an attractive option for homosexuals seeking to adopt? *Indiana Journal of Global Legal Studies, 6*(1), 237.
Tasker, F., & Golombok, S. (1998). The role of co-mothers in planned lesbian-led families. *Journal of Lesbian Studies, 2*(4), 49–68.

QUESTIONS FOR DISCUSSION

1. What were the most important things for Ann to keep in mind as she worked with Lucy and Rob while they were going through the process of assisted insemination?

2. In what ways might the insemination process have been different for Lucy and Rob?

3. What impact would the insemination process likely have had on Lucy and Rob's relationship?

4. What are the most important issues for Rob as she contemplates either Lucy's pregnancy or the decision about pursuing adoption as an open lesbian couple?

5. Given the Hague Convention, what advice would Carol Halbertson give Lucy and Rob? (Note: The specific provisions and regulations of the Hague Convention are not fully clear at this writing; to answer this question it will be necessary to gather current information about the policy. The Internet is the most likely source for up-to-date information.)

6. How would the advice that Carol Halbertson gives Lucy and Rob affect the emotional issues that they are continuing to discuss with Ann?

POLICY-RELATED QUESTIONS

1. Is the United States a signator to the Hague Convention?

2. What is the current interpretation of the Hague Convention as to the rights of adoption by lesbian and gay couples?

3. Does the state in which you live have legislation that protects the civil rights of GLBT populations?

4. If the answer to the previous question is yes, what are the implications for Lucy and Rob of the civil rights legislation in your state to the restrictions imposed by the Hague Convention?

EXERCISE

Name: Finding the Resources to Be a Good Social Worker

Purpose: To identify resources in the community for providing services to GLBT families; to identify the range of social work intervention issues to be addressed in terms of adoption and usual remedies; to develop greater sensitivity to the unique issues of GLBT families; to apply assessment skills to GLBT family issues

Structure: Students will work in small groups to identify appropriate resources to assist the clients in the case study. They will begin the research before they come to class, and then they will review their findings, first in small groups and finally in the larger class.

Implementation: One to two weeks before conducting this exercise, the class will be divided into groups of five or six students. Half of the groups will take the role of Ann Foster and the other half will take the role of Carol Halbertson. All students will read the case and explore resources that would assist them in carrying out the responsibilities of their role. Various resources might include the text, the attached references, local and national directories of adoption service agencies, and the Internet (among others that instructors may identify).

On the day of the exercise, members of each group will meet and develop responses to the following questions:

1. What are your responsibilities to Lucy and Rob in addressing their questions/concerns about international adoption?
2. What are the resources available to you in meeting each of those responsibilities?
3. What resources/referrals are available to Lucy and Rob as they pursue international adoption? What specific advice, contacts, and/or referrals would you give to Lucy and Rob if they were a couple in your community?
4. What are your responsibilities to the other professionals who will be working with Lucy and Rob as they begin and carry out the adoption process?

Groups will meet for 20–30 minutes, and each one will select a recorder who will present the group's answers to the class.

When the groups reconvene, the recorders of each will present their conclusions to the whole class. The class will discuss the differences and similarities in responsibilities and resources identified as appropriate to the two different roles. This discussion should last 20–30 minutes.

Suggested Social Work Courses: Any direct service methods course

Suggested Class Size: Class size of 10–12 would be ideal for two small groups of 5–6 members each. Alternatively, larger classes may be divided into several small groups of 4–6 members, with multiple groups assuming each professional role.

Materials and Time: Newsprint or other large area for recording/displaying results of small- and large-group discussions. Small-group discussions should consume no more than half of the available class time (up to 30 minutes); large-group discussion may be conducted in 30 minutes or within the remaining time available.

17

MAKING DIFFICULT DECISIONS

Harriet L. Cohen

ELLEN AND LEAH, both 64 years old, have been together for more than thirty years. They proudly present themselves as an interfaith couple who have created a spiritual home not only for themselves but for friends as well.

The daughter of a minister, Ellen was raised in a traditional Christian home with church activities and responsibilities several times a week. She heard the Bible preached in church and at home, and while she found some comfort in the prayers and the music, she felt limited by the theology and boundaries of her parents' religion. Unlike some of her women friends who found traditional Christianity too patriarchal, Ellen explored various Christian churches until she located a religious community that she experienced as loving and consistent with her views of the divine, human relationships, and ministry. Before she met Leah, Ellen was active in the church, attending worship regularly and serving as a teacher, mentor, and choir member. Since they have been together, Leah and Ellen have attended church services and church functions together and are recognized and respected as an interfaith lesbian couple. They have many friends at the church, including straight, gay, and lesbian couples.

Leah was raised Jewish in the South and was heavily influenced by the activism and leadership of her rabbi and members of the Jewish community in fighting for civil rights and social and economic justice for all. She continues to be active in her synagogue and in the Jewish community. She has worked professionally in the Jewish community and served in leadership positions in various Jewish social service organizations and synagogues. In her earlier years, she helped develop rituals for Jewish women's groups. Ellen occasionally attends services with Leah and participates actively in the celebration of Jewish holidays and rituals in their home.

As an interfaith couple, Leah and Ellen have brought their spiritual paths into the relationship. They developed what they lovingly referred to as their "Jewish, Episcopal, New Age, inclusive language" service to welcome the Jewish Sabbath on Friday evenings. Their home and their dinner table have provided safe and sacred places where people of various religious backgrounds and beliefs can come together and experience the divine presence through love, laughter, friendship, and healthy food. Leah and Ellen continue to facilitate interfaith discussion groups and workshops helping people to explore their own spiritual paths, transcending differences among people who identified with diverse religious traditions.

Leah was recently diagnosed with breast cancer, which has provided the opportunity for the two of them to discuss death and burial, a subject that they have talked about intermittently over the years but without any clear resolution. Now, however, they have begun to explore their religious and spiritual beliefs about the subject in more depth and have identified distinctions in their theology and practices that they find troubling and irreconcilable. Ellen would like to be cremated and have her ashes planted in the gardens at her church. Since neither she nor Leah has children, she does not feel that she needs a "place" for her body, only a home for her ashes.

Leah does not support the concept of cremation, since it is contrary to Jewish tradition for a Jew to be cremated. Also, Leah feels that cremation demonstrates disrespect to the Jews and gays and lesbians who were killed by cremation during the Holocaust. Leah wants to be buried in a Jewish cemetery, and yet at the same time she wants Ellen and herself to be buried as a couple. While the synagogue to which Leah belongs does allow non-Jewish people to be buried in the adjoining cemetery, Ellen does not want to be buried there. Another part of the issue for Leah is that she has always considered herself an environmentalist and is struggling with the idea that burial uses land that could be reserved for nature. Leah is considering donating her body to one of the medical schools in the area. If she does so, then her body will be cremated. She will have to decide whether she wants to be cremated and have her ashes buried with the other bodies donated to science or whether she would ask one of her nieces or nephews to receive her ashes from the medical school and spread them in one of her favorite nature spots. Another option for Leah would be to donate her body to science and then have her ashes interred in the gardens surrounding the church where Ellen wants her ashes buried.

The different rituals related to death and dying in the couple's traditions are also a factor. The Jewish faith has very clearly defined rituals, including specified times of mourning and certain prayers that are said in community. Since Ellen is not Jewish, the women are concerned that if Leah dies before Ellen does, Ellen will not find a community to say the Jewish prayers to honor their relationship. If Ellen dies first, they worry that Leah will not have a community in which to share the prayers to remember her non-Jewish partner.

A further and complicating challenge involves their larger families. Leah's family has been openly accepting and welcoming of Leah and Ellen's relationship for the past thirty years and has celebrated many anniversaries and special occasions with Ellen and Leah as a loving couple. Ellen, on the other hand, has not discussed the relationship with her family because of their strong fundamentalist Christian values. While Leah has for many years been included in Ellen's family get-togethers, the question of how their relationship will be presented at the funeral presents a spiritual dilemma for them as a couple. Since they have created a chosen family of friends, they want their funeral services to be consistent with their deeply held values and to represent the spiritual life that they have created together. However, they do not want to hurt Ellen's family at the time of the funeral with the acknowledgment and recognition of the depth of love, care, respect, and devotion that they have shared during the thirty years of their committed relationship.

CORRESPONDING TEXTBOOK CHAPTERS

Chapter 10: Lesbian relationships and families, by C. A. Parks & N. A. Humphreys.
Chapter 13: Gay, lesbian, bisexual, and transgender older people, by E. M. Fullmer.
Chapter 17: Religion and spirituality, by D. F. Morrow & B. Tyson.

ADDITIONAL READINGS

Aish HaTorah (a nonprofit, apolitical, international network of Jewish educational centers). http://www.aish.com/literacy/lifecycle/The_Stages_of_Jewish_Mourning.asp http://www.aish.com/literacy/lifecycle/The_Jewish_Way_of_Mourning.asp http://www.aish.com/family/rebbitzen/Sensitivity_Training.asp

Barranti, C. C. R., & Cohen, H. L. (2000). Lesbian and gay elders: An invisible minority. In R. L. Schneider, N. P. Kropf, & Anne Kisor (Eds.), *Gerontological social work: Knowledge, service settings, and special populations* (2nd ed.). Belmont, CA: Wadsworth/Thomson Learning.

Curry, H., Clifford, D., & Hertz, F. (2002). *A legal guide for lesbians and gay couples* (11th ed.). Berkeley, CA: Nolo Press.

Isaacs, R. H. (1999). *Every person's guide to death and dying in the Jewish tradition.* New York: Jason Aronson, 1999.

Jones, T. C., & Nystrom, N. M. (2002). Looking back … looking forward: Addressing the lives of lesbians 55 and older. *Journal of Women and Aging, 14*(3/4), 59–76.

Kimmel, D. C. (1992). Families of older gay men and lesbians. *Generations, 17*(3), 37–38.

Lesbian and Gay Aging Issues Network. http://www.asaging.org/lgain/.

SAGE (Senior Action in a Gay Environment). http://www.sageusa.org.

Westerberg-Reyes, K. (Ed.). (1994). *Lambda gray: A practical, emotional and spiritual guide for gays and lesbians who are growing older.* North Hollywood, CA: Newcastle Publishing.

Wolowelsky, J. B. (1996). Communal and individual mourning dynamics within traditional Jewish law. *Death Studies, 20*(5), 469–480.

QUESTIONS FOR DISCUSSION

1. What resources are necessary to help Ellen and Leah make difficult decisions about where to be buried?

2. If they choose different locations, how will that affect their current relationship?

3. If they choose to be buried together, what compromises will each have to make?

4. How can they develop a meaningful funeral service that will not be hurtful to Ellen's family?

5. Since neither the Jewish nor the Christian community in which they are involved formally recognizes lesbian relationships, how will they develop meaningful rituals that will bring comfort to the mourning partner?

6. What social work intervention(s) are most appropriate for Ellen and Leah's situation? What research guides your decisions?

EXERCISE

Name: Planning for Your Death

Purpose: To provide students an opportunity to think about their issues, feelings, and reactions concerning death before they begin to work with clients. To help them to explore their values, rituals, and beliefs about dying, death, and bereavement. To expose them to conflicts that might arise for a lesbian couple, living with an invisible identity, at the time of a loved one's death.

Structure: Individual assignment at home, individual work in the class, small-group discussion, and large-group discussion about implications for social work practice

Implementation: Students will complete a durable power of attorney and living will for their state before they come to class. Most states have copies or sample forms of the medical power of attorney available on the Internet. Students can do a Google search for "durable power of attorney for health care." The AARP Web site (www.aarp.org) provides good definitions of all advance directive documents.

When students arrive in class, they will receive Handout I. They will complete the questions individually, limiting their conversation while working (15 minutes).

Handout II will be distributed. The class will divide into small groups of 3–5 for discussion using Handout II and reaction to the exercise (30 minutes).

Returning to the large classroom setting, the students will discuss the following questions: What issues, feelings, and reactions came up in exploring their cultural, religious/spiritual, and family issues with regard to dying and death? What strengths and concerns do they have in addressing these issues with clients? Do they feel they could speak with a lesbian or gay couple about these issues? What additional information or experience do they need in order to be comfortable exploring death and dying issues with an interfaith lesbian couple? What did they learn from the experience that will assist them in their social work practice? (15 minutes).

Suggested Social Work Courses: Undergraduate or graduate HBSE; practice/methods; cultural diversity; spirituality and religion; mental health; aging; death and dying; practicum seminar

Suggested Class Size: This exercise can work with any size class; because of the intimate nature of the material being discussed, however, it is important to keep the groups small.

Materials and Time: Two handouts. The exercise should take one hour.

HANDOUT I: INDIVIDUAL REFLECTION ON PERSONAL, FAMILY, CULTURAL, AND RELIGIOUS/ SPIRITUAL BELIEFS AND PRACTICE ABOUT DYING AND DEATH

1. What are your values with regard to dying, death, mourning, and bereavement? How are your values influenced by the culture and/or by your religious or spiritual beliefs and practices?

2. Do you want to be buried? Do you want to be cremated? Explain your decision.

3. What rituals of death and dying are important to you? What rituals will be important to your family and friends? How will you reconcile any differences between what you want and what your family or friends want or need?

4. What additional issues might come up for you if part of your identity has been invisible to your family or friends?

5. What values or qualities will people remember about you? Is this how you want to be remembered?

HANDOUT II: SMALL-GROUP REFLECTIVE QUESTIONS ON DYING AND DEATH

1. What were your feelings and reactions to completing the durable power of attorney for health care and the living will?

2. What issues came up for you in planning your own funeral?

3. What additional issues might come up for you with regard to living with an invisible identity?

4. Do the decisions and choices you are making in your daily life reflect the values and beliefs that you want others to remember about you?

18

JACK AND KAREN: A TRANSGENDER LOVE STORY

Carolyn A. Bradley

JACK'S PHYSICIAN has referred Jack and his wife, Karen, for therapy. At age 36, Jack has high blood pressure, peptic ulcers, and elevated liver enzymes. His medical conditions are secondary to active alcoholism and cocaine and marijuana use.

Jack and Karen are a white middle-class couple living in a suburban town in the Northeast. Karen, age 34, has been married to Jack for sixteen years. They met in high school, where Jack was on the football team and Karen was a cheerleader. Both came from homes in which the parents were active alcoholics. Karen saw Jack as her hero, who got her out of the house and away from her verbally and physically abusive father.

Both of Jack's parents were alcoholics. His father was a quiet daily drinker who came home from work and drank until he passed out in his chair. His mother, also a daily drinker, was verbally and physically abusive to her husband and her children.

Karen has never known Jack clean and sober. He started drinking at age 12, while in middle school. He began marijuana use at age 15. His cocaine use began in college around age 20.

Increasingly Karen is disturbed by Jack's use of substances. She has worked throughout their marriage in order to provide a source of steady and predictable income. Despite Karen's efforts, the family is experiencing serious financial problems. Karen has watched Jack develop and lose several businesses. Currently, Jack's window and siding business is in danger of folding, just as his deli business did and his boat canvas and awning business before that. Jack's side business of growing marijuana in the attic of their home, which he refers to as the Secret Garden, is also problematic for Karen.

Jack and Karen's marriage has deteriorated seriously. They have three children, two boys and a girl, ages 10, 7, and 4. Jack spends a great deal of time out of the home.

The couple are no longer emotionally or sexually intimate. They have never been extremely sexual with each other. Jack is affectionate and caring when he is sober. He is very romantic and thoughtful, sending cards, bringing flowers, and so on. He has always had difficulty maintaining an erection for intercourse. The couple enjoys oral sex. Jack engages in intercourse most successfully when he is high on cocaine.

Jack can be verbally and physically threatening to Karen and the children when he is drunk or high. The police have been to the home on several occasions for domestic violence complaints.

Karen no longer sees Jack as her hero. She is disillusioned and at times afraid of him. She wants "the Secret Garden" business shut down and removed from the house. She holds on to her memories of what their early years were like. She lives in the past, denies the present, and hopes for a better future.

Jack has attempted sobriety several times but always relapses. He has been in outpatient and inpatient programs. He has attended AA. He says he is ready to try anything at this point. Jack doesn't want to lose his wife, his children, his legitimate business, and possibly his life.

Jack and Karen entered into therapy. They were seen in couples, family, and individual sessions. Jack went to AA and Karen went to Al-Anon. Jack would get sober, stay sober briefly, and then relapse.

Jack presents as very sincere in his desire to achieve sobriety. He feels immense guilt for what Karen and the children have been through as a result of his substance abuse. In individual sessions he speaks about not wanting to duplicate for his children the type of home environment in which he grew up.

When Jack is sober, the couple's sexual relations problems are a major issue. Jack loses weight when he is sober. He feels good about his physical appearance. He wants to have sex with Karen, and Karen is agreeable. She describes Jack as a tender and attentive partner. But Jack can't maintain an erection. Karen suggests that this is not a problem for her. She feels that there are other means by which they can both be satisfied. Neither partner wants additional children. Jack, however, becomes frustrated and angry about this issue, and shortly after that happens, he relapses.

In tracking this issue through a relapse scenario in an individual session with Jack, the secret comes out. Jack identifies himself as "a cross-dresser." The constant relapsing with the accompanying weight gain serves as a protective factor against the cross-dressing. It is hard to locate women's clothing to fit a six-three, 230-pound frame. During a relapse, Jack's weight will climb as high as 280 pounds.

Jack feels great shame about what he sees as a problem for himself and his marriage. When he wants to attempt to have sex, he secretly dresses as a woman before initiating any sexual contact. Jack would enjoy dressing as a woman most of the time. He shares how he feels as though he should be a woman but is happy also as a man. Jack feels that he can't share this side of himself with Karen. Having been raised Irish Catholic, he feels that his behavior is sinful and grounds for annulment in the Church and a civil divorce.

With significant work on exploring what constitutes "normal" sexual practices between consenting adults, additional reading on Jack's part, and participation in gay and lesbian AA meetings, Jack is able to self-identify as a transgender person. He is very much at ease with feelings and behaviors that are culturally assigned to women. He is not interested in becoming a woman through sex reassignment surgery. He wants to learn how to live comfortably and successfully as a transgender person.

With the support of his therapist, Jack "comes out" as a transgender person to Karen in a joint session. Karen is very accepting and grateful for the disclosure. She has been afraid that there was another woman in Jack's life. Jack and Karen over time make a joke that the other woman was really Jack. Karen is accepting of Jack's cross-dressing before having sexual relations.

After eighteen months of continuous sobriety, Jack and Karen are referred to a therapist who specializes in adjustment to transgender living. Jack continues in the fellowship of the lesbian and gay AA. He has maintained continuous sobriety for five years now, is still married to Karen, no longer has "the Secret Garden," and successfully manages his own business. The health issues that precipitated the referral for therapy have been resolved.

CORRESPONDING TEXTBOOK CHAPTERS

Chapter 5: Transgender identity, by J. I. Martin & D. R. Yonkin.
Chapter 6: Coming out as gay, lesbian, bisexual, and transgender, by D. F. Morrow.
Chapter 12: Transgender emergence within families, by A. I. Lev.

ADDITIONAL READINGS

Canda, E. R., & Furman, L. D. (1999). *Spiritual diversity in social work practice*. New York: Free Press.
Devor, H. (1989). *Gender bending*. Bloomington: Indiana University Press.
McGoldrick, M. (Ed.). (1998). *Revisioning family therapy*. New York: Guilford.
Miller, M., Gorski, T., & Miller, D. (1992). *Learning to live again*. Independence, MO: Herald House.
Mollenkott, V. R. (2001). *Omnigender*. Cleveland: Pilgrim Press.
Reamer, F. G. (1999). *Social work values and ethics*. New York: Columbia University Press.

QUESTIONS FOR DISCUSSION

1. How would you pursue relapse prevention work with this family?

2. What ethical and legal issues are involved in this case, given Jack's disclosure of the secret in an individual session rather than a joint session?

3. How would you develop a comprehensive outpatient treatment plan for Jack and Karen to rebalance the relationship in sobriety?

4. What issues does Karen bring as an adult child of an abusive alcoholic that may have contributed to her accepting Jack's long-term substance abuse?

5. How would you define the terms *sex, gender, sexual orientation, gender expression, heterosexual, homosexual, bisexual,* and *transgender*?

6. What is the impact of culturally defined male and female behavior and roles on Jack and Karen's marriage?

EXERCISE

Name: Case Plan to Address Clients' Spiritual and Religious Needs

Purpose: To develop awareness of the need to examine issues of spirituality and religion in recovering clients and with GLBT clients

Structure: Students use a list of questions to frame small-group discussion. After discussing these questions, students develop a case plan for their clients. Student report on their case plans.

Implementation: Students will read the case study (5 minutes), then move into small groups of three to six each. The instructor will give each group a copy of the discussion questions. The small groups will discuss the case and develop a case plan (10 minutes). The whole class will then reconvene, and each small group will share its plan (15 minutes).

Suggested Social Work Courses: Family practice, ethics, substance abuse

Suggested Class Size: 25 maximum

Materials and Time: Copies of the case and discussion questions for each class member. This exercise should last approximately 30 minutes.

HANDOUT: QUESTIONS FOR DISCUSSION

1. What religious and spiritual topics need to be explored with these clients?

2. What are the ethical considerations for the social worker in exploring these issues?

3. Should the social worker involve or consult clergy?

4. Should the clients be referred to clergy?

5. Should the issue be explored with only Jack or with Jack and Karen as a couple?

19

"WHO'S YOUR DADDY?"

Lori Messinger

THIS CASE involves Mark Johnson, an adoptions worker at Laredo Child and Family Services in Texas, and his work with newly adoptive parents Jonathon and Fernando, who had recently adopted two special-needs children. In adjusting to their new roles as parents, the couple had begun to experience conflict.

THE PHONE CALL

"Hello, Mark Johnson speaking, how can I help you?" Mark spoke quickly, eyeing the clock on the wall and gathering his papers for the staff meeting scheduled to begin in five minutes.

"Hi. It is Jonathon Getz. Got a minute?"

"Just a minute, really," Mark replied. "I'm on my way to a meeting."

"Maybe we can make an appointment to meet, then," stammered Jonathon.

"Are the kids okay?" Mark asked, referring to the two children he had helped Jonathon adopt.

"Yeah, they're doing great. It's Fernando and me." Jonathon sighed. "We're really having a hard time adjusting. I just need to talk about it."

Mark and Jonathon made an appointment to meet for an hour the next week. "And bring Fernando, too, if he is available," suggested Mark.

"I'll see if he can make it," responded Jonathon. "See you then."

Mark Johnson hung up the telephone and made a notation in his calendar for the appointment. He was concerned that there seemed to be such a quick onset of trouble in the family. He had worked hard to help Jonathon and Fernando with the adoption process for Thomas Mendez, 5, and his sister Juliana, 2. Mark remembered being nervous when he first interviewed Jonathon and Fernando. As a 31-year-old heterosexual social worker, Mark had had little interaction with gay men or lesbians in his professional or personal life. He felt unsure of how to effectively serve them, and he contemplated transferring the couple to another worker. Yet his unit, which oversaw adoptions for difficult-to-place children, was small and no other worker was better prepared than he to deal with this "nontraditional" couple.

The day he reviewed Jonathon and Fernando's application materials, Mark had been surprised to find they possessed more strengths than many of the agency's heterosexual applicants. Jonathon Getz, 40, and Fernando Estrada, 39, were partners in a long-term relationship of more than ten years. They were in good health, owned a large house together in a vibrant neighborhood, and had already decided that Fernando would be the primary at-home caretaker for the children when Jonathon was at work. Mark noted that both Jonathon and Fernando were fluent in Spanish—the first language of both children—and Fernando was from Costa Rica, the same country as that of the children's biological family.

Mark had informed Jonathon and Fernando at their first meeting that as a gay couple in Laredo, Texas, they could not both serve as legally adoptive parents for the children; under current state law and agency policy, one or the other would have to be the designated legal parent. The couple decided that Jonathon, as a U.S. citizen and business owner, would have the best chance of being approved as the "official" adoptive parent. Thus the adoption proceeded with Jonathon as the legal parent.

THE MEETING

As Mark prepared for his meeting with Jonathon, he thought about the two children, Thomas and Juliana. Both had been in foster care for most of their lives. Each of them had special needs—Thomas struggled with a learning disability and a speech impediment that impaired his communication skills in English and Spanish, and Juliana suffered from developmental delays and health problems related to fetal alcohol syndrome. Their energy and needs were sure to keep the two new parents very busy. "Perhaps Jonathon and Fernando are experiencing typical adjustment stress," Mark reasoned. "Just the initial shock of accommodating two special-needs children into their lives is tremendous, and it's only been three months since the adoption."

Both Jonathon and Fernando arrived on time at Mark's office for the meeting. Mark could sense the tension in the air as he shook their hands and invited them in to sit down. Jonathon took a place on the couch facing Mark, while Fernando sat in a chair far away in the corner.

Mark opened the discussion by smiling and asking the men, "So, what's up?"

Fernando glared at Jonathon, who answered, "Well, as I said on the phone, we are really happy to have the kids, but we can't stop fighting."

"Bringing children into your lives is certainly stressful," Mark responded. "It's normal for new parents to struggle a little, especially when the children have special needs."

Jonathon said, "I think we have adjusted to caring for the children, but something has changed in our relationship. We just can't seem to agree on anything."

"What are you disagreeing about?" Mark asked.

"How to relate to the kids, to each other," Jonathon replied. "I think he resents me being the dad, even though we had to do it that way."

Mark turned to Fernando, inviting him into the discussion. "How do you view the problem, Fernando?"

"I understand why Jon was the one to legally adopt the children." Fernando shrugged. "But he doesn't want them to call me Papa. He wants them to call me Fernando. I think that is crazy, for children to call a father by his name. It is wrong."

"But there can only be one father and that's me," argued Jonathon. "I mean, I am the one who legally adopted the children."

"You see?" exclaimed Fernando, throwing a hand in the air. "You see what I live with. Who am I, then? Am I not a parent too?"

"Of course you are a parent, Fernando, just not their father," stated Jonathon. His words hung in the air as the three men pondered one another. Jonathon blushed and sighed. "Oh, I don't know what you are." He turned to Mark and said, "I just feel like Fernando is pushing me all the time. It is like he doesn't get enough attention now that we have the children."

"What exactly do you mean?" asked Mark.

"Well, he practically hangs all over me when I come home from work. It's like he forgets the children are there—kissing and touching me, like we did before we adopted them." Jonathon, embarrassed, looked at his hands, which were clasped in his lap.

Fernando responded, "What is wrong with affection between parents? Didn't your mother and father show affection to each other?"

"We're not my parents!" Jonathon said angrily, moving forward in his chair. "Fernando, you just don't understand!"

"Jon, can you help Fernando understand what you mean?" Mark asked gently.

"It's just wrong." Jonathon sank back into his chair.

"What is wrong?" Mark probed again.

"Listen, I know I shouldn't be saying this," Jonathon said quietly, glancing at Fernando and then looking closely at Mark, "because I don't want to lose the kids. But when he touches me, it just seems too gay to me. In front of the kids, that is. It just can't be good for them to see that, right?"

Mark squirmed uncomfortably in his chair, feeling the two men looking at him. He was surprised, in a way, that they were having these problems. After all of the assessment and the discussions they had had about parenting, it had seemed to Mark that this couple was well prepared for the adoption. Now, looking at their angry and confused faces, he was not so sure.

"I don't really know what to say," Mark admitted. "This is outside my area of expertise. I can help with the children and their care, but it sounds to me like you two have some relationship issues to work through. Perhaps you might talk to a therapist about this?"

Fernando looked at Jonathon, who nodded sheepishly.

"Yes," said Fernando, leaning forward and taking Jonathon's hand. "Yes, I think we should do that. Do you know someone we could talk to?"

Mark moved to his desk and pulled out his Rolodex. "Um, let me see." He flipped through several cards, finally pausing at one and nodding. "Yes. Janice Roderstam. She was a colleague of mine from school, a lesbian. I don't know her that well, but I know that she does couples therapy. Would you be comfortable talking to a woman?"

The two men agreed that they would be fine with the referral. Mark wrote her name and number on a small slip of paper and handed it to Jonathon.

"Please let me know if you have any concerns about your children," Mark offered.

Jonathon paused at the door and asked, "Would you come with us, the first time, to meet with that therapist? I mean, you just know us so well."

"Sure, if that is okay with both of you," he said, turning also to Fernando. Fernando nodded.

They agreed to schedule the first session at a time convenient for all of them, and they made the appointment before leaving Mark's office. The couple thanked Mark and walked to the door together, their hands clasped.

CORRESPONDING TEXTBOOK CHAPTERS

Chapter 4: Gay, lesbian, and bisexual identity development, by D. F. Morrow.
Chapter 9: Gay male relationships and families, by R. E. McKinney.
Chapter 19: Social welfare policy and advocacy, by L. Messinger.

ADDITIONAL READINGS

Baptiste, D. A. (1987). Psychotherapy with gay/lesbian couples and their children in "stepfamilies": A challenge for marriage and family therapists. *Journal of Homosexuality, 14*(1–2), 223–238.
Bigner, J. J. (1999). Raising our sons: Gay men as fathers. *Journal of Gay and Lesbian Social Services, 10*(1), 61.
Bozett, F. W. (Ed.). (1987). *Gay and lesbian parents*. New York: Praeger.
Brooks, D., & Goldberg, S. (2001). Gay and lesbian adoptive and foster care placements: Can they meet the needs of waiting children? *Social Work, 46*(2), 147–157.
Cass, V. C. (1979). Homosexual identity formation: A theoretical model. *Journal of Homosexuality, 4*(3), 219–235.

QUESTIONS FOR DISCUSSION

1. What is the presenting problem in this case? What are the primary issues?

2. What is the impact of internalized homophobia on this couple? How is it manifested?

3. How might the legal issues involved in becoming parents (as a gay couple) affect this couple's sense of power and value as parents?

4. Using the Cass model of gay identity development (Cass, 1979), determine at what stage Fernando and Jonathon are. How might the model explain some of the conflict between the two men?

5. If you were Janice, the therapist to whom the couple has been referred, what information would you need from this couple to understand their conflicts?

6. Is it appropriate to refer this couple to a lesbian therapist? Is it necessary?

7. How might the cultural background of each client affect his feelings about parenting? About public displays of affection?

8. Was there something Mark should have included in his assessment that might have helped to identify and address these issues before the adoption? In what ways was his assessment limited by agency and state policies?

EXERCISE

Name: Counseling Jigsaw/Role-Play

Purpose: To help students better understand the perspectives of the clients and the social workers who are working with them

Structure: Students divide into four groups, each representing a person in this case: (1) Mark, (2) Fernando, (3) Jonathon, and (4) Janice. This exercise will proceed in two stages. First, "like groups" (that is, all of the 1s) will meet and identify their assigned person's perspective. Next, students divide into "unlike groups," each consisting of four different people: one Jonathon, one Fernando, one Mark, and one Janice. Students then role-play the first session in which the earlier identified issues are discussed. At the conclusion, students may then discuss their reactions to their experiences in the exercises.

Implementation: Students will "count off" by fours. The instructor will explain that each number represents a person in this scenario: Number 1s are Jonathon, number 2s are Fernando, and so on. The students will break into the "like groups" by numbers and talk with the others, who will play the same part about the person's needs, perspectives, plans for the session, and so on. This part of the activity will require approximately 10 minutes.

While the small groups are meeting, the instructor will pass out sets of slips of paper with letters on them, one set for each number group. Each member of the number group should get a different letter. (Any extra people may become observers in the role-plays.) When the students finish the initial discussion, they will break into letter groups for the role-play, with each letter group assigned to a section of the room. After about 15 minutes the class will reassemble to process the exercise, which may last 15–20 minutes.

Suggested Social Work Courses: Direct practice with individuals and families; clinical work with couples; clinical work with families; clinical work with gay men and lesbians

Suggested Class Size: 12–36 students

Materials and Time: Four sets of slips of paper with letters on them, corresponding to the number of groups appropriate for the class size, and movable desks. The exercise will last 40–45 minutes.

PART THREE

GROUPS

THE THREE chapters in this section deal with a support group (chapter 20) and collections of clients who share similar characteristics (chapters 21 and 22). When reading chapter 20, students can examine the use of group work with GLBT people, and then they can consider how they would conduct groups with the people involved in chapters 21 and 22.

The characters in each of the chapters are diverse—racially, ethnically, culturally, and socioeconomically. Instructors can use these differences to challenge students to consider the differences and their impact on individual and group work with these clients and their social support systems.

It is also important for students to consider the impact of micro-, mezzo-, and macro-level forces on the individuals discussed in these chapters. The women described in chapter 20 are negotiating their family, school, and community relationships. The homeless youths described in chapter 21 confront family dysfunction, discriminatory institutional policies, a local culture of drugs and prostitution that preys on homeless youths, poverty, and homophobia. The transgender people in chapter 22 must negotiate social, workplace, and medical settings—all while confronting society's expectations about gender expression and gender identity. Each of these factors must be considered along with the characters' individual strengths and weaknesses.

20

THE DAY WE SHARED OUR COMING OUT STORIES

Elizabeth Cramer

THE COZY room at the gay and lesbian community center was filling up fast, since it was nearly seven in the evening. One facilitator, LaTonya, was greeting members and making a point to spend some extra time with those women who were new to the group. Becky, the other facilitator, was busy taping the group guidelines to the wall. There was some boisterous chatter among old friends in the group and quiet contemplation among the new members.

It was time to begin. After introductions, a review of group guidelines, and a member check-in, the facilitators introduced a topic for the evening: our coming out stories, or how we came to identify ourselves as lesbian, bisexual, transgender, or questioning. There were some smiles, some giggles, some confused expressions on faces. To help get the discussion started, and to model group norms and culture for the new members, LaTonya began by telling her story.

"God blessed me by making me black and making me gay," she said. LaTonya said that she "just knew" she was gay back in elementary school when she realized she had a crush on another schoolgirl. This scared and confused her because she heard people talk about the "bulldaggers" in the neighborhood and the men in choir who were "funny," and they didn't sound like it was something positive. LaTonya kept her feelings in check until her freshman year in high school. She met a girl in her English class, Alesha, who played on the basketball team and looked like what folks called "mannish." LaTonya thought she was real cute. Alesha was always making jokes that made LaTonya laugh. LaTonya began to attend basketball games regularly. She loved to watch the strong and active girls—this excited her—but then she would feel ashamed of herself for those feelings. She wondered to herself: Am I a homosexual?

Eventually LaTonya and Alesha shared a quick kiss one evening when listening to music over at Alesha's house. LaTonya thought to herself, "I like this. I like this a whole lot. I think this must mean that I really am homosexual." LaTonya and Alesha began a relationship that lasted through their junior year in high school. By that time, Alesha's family had been pressuring her to date boys. LaTonya's parents were happy that LaTonya did not seem interested in boys. They assumed LaTonya had more important things in her life than dating. Alesha was buckling under the pressure. She began to date a boy from the boys' basketball team, Willie. Alesha pushed LaTonya away and said that they could not be intimate anymore, and in fact it might be better if they just kept some distance from each other. LaTonya was devastated.

In college, LaTonya joined the gay and lesbian student association. She told the group members, "I guess those were my militant years because everything was about being gay—gay this, gay that." During those years she met many other "queer folks" and participated in several gay pride rallies and marches. She laughed and told the group: "Hey, I guess I needed to go through that to accept who I am today. Now, five years after I graduated college and 27 years old, I don't have to get in anyone's face to say 'I'm gay, get used to it.' Being gay is just one part of me. I'm also a black female. I'm a Christian. I'm an avid reader. I love to dance. I did tell my parents that I'm gay when I was in college. I kind of regret the way I told them because I shoved it down their throats. They had a hard time with it at first, but now they are all right with it. Well, they would prefer that it not get talked about, actually." LaTonya smiled and asked who was ready to tell her story.

Margaret volunteered to go next. "But I wasn't as sure as you, LaTonya, and I'm still not." She looked down at the floor and then slowly raised her eyes to look around the room. There was some nodding, so she thought she wasn't the only one whose journey had been different from LaTonya's. Margaret shared that she didn't really have feelings of same-sex attraction until after she was married to a man. She grew up in a traditional family in a rural area, surrounded by other white families like hers. It was expected that she would marry out of high school. Margaret fulfilled familial expectations by marrying Chuck at age 19. Now that she was 24, with two young children, she wondered how she managed to get herself into this. She loved Chuck and her kids, but something felt like it was missing in her life.

Margaret said to the group, "I regretted that I never even considered college. I was a good student in high school. With my husband's support, I decided to take college courses part-time." Attending college classes exposed Margaret to an array of people and ideas that were very different from her small-town upbringing. She was pushed beyond her comfort zone many times. She often contemplated whether she belonged in the academic environment, yet she received positive feedback about her work and earned high grades. Although she was not much older than the other students, she could not relate to many of them because they were not married and parenting.

During her second year of taking college courses, Margaret took an introduction to women's studies course. "I tell y'all," she said to the group, "I was worried I would be in there with a bunch of man-haters!" The course turned Margaret's life upside down. During one of the class sessions, the instructor showed a clip of a popular film, *The Incredibly True Adventure of 2 Girls in Love*. The two young actresses in the film were being intimate in the bedroom of one of the girls, and the mother of the girl walked in. Margaret had a riot of emotions whirling inside her as she watched. She was at once repulsed by and attracted to the intimacy displayed by the two girls. She felt empathy for the mother who walked in on her daughter and thought about how she would feel if she caught her own daughter engaging in that behavior. After the clip, the instructor asked for reactions from the students. After a few seconds of silence, which seemed like an eternity to Margaret, a young woman in the class raised her hand and said that she too had been "caught" by a parent while kissing her girlfriend. That broke the ice and people started to smile and laugh.

Margaret told herself to approach the brave young woman after class and express her appreciation for her sharing with the class. "I was so nervous to go up to her," she told the group members. Class ended, and Margaret tentatively walked up to Laura, a 20-year-old white lesbian. She introduced herself and complimented Laura on her courage. Laura asked Margaret if she had a class right then and if not, would she like to go to the student commons and grab a bite to eat? Margaret said she had about forty-five minutes before she needed to get the kids from her mother's house. Over a meal at the commons Laura and Margaret talked about their lives. Laura invited Margaret to a potluck dinner at a friend's house the following week. Margaret said she would need to get back to her on that because she needed to check with her husband first.

"I didn't know whether I should tell Chuck about the invitation," she said to the women in group. Should she tell him that a woman she'd just met from her class had asked her to go to a potluck dinner and that this woman was a lesbian? She figured Chuck wouldn't understand why she would want to spend time with someone who was a lesbian and he would wonder if all the other people at the potluck would also be homosexuals. Margaret had never lied to Chuck, and she didn't want to start now. That night, after putting the kids to bed, Margaret told Chuck she had something to tell him. She told him about the class, the film clip, the brave student, the meal after class, and the invitation to the potluck. Chuck looked at Margaret and said, "You've got to be kidding, right?" Margaret said, "No, darlin', I'm not kidding. Would it bother you if I went? I feel so out of place at school and maybe this is a way for me to meet other students." "But why do you want to meet homosexuals?" Chuck asked. Margaret explained that she thought her upbringing had made her close-minded to people and there was a whole world out there that she hardly knew. This was a way to help open her mind more. Chuck reluctantly agreed that Margaret should go to the potluck dinner. She disclosed to the group members, "I think if he knew that this potluck would be the start of me wondering who I am, he might not have agreed for me to go that night."

Margaret pondered what a married woman with children should bring to a potluck where there might be a whole lot of lesbians. "I didn't want to seem old-fashioned and 'country,'" she joked with the group. She finally decided on her mama's macaroni-and-cheese recipe. She figured she couldn't go too wrong with that. Laura offered to pick her up at the house and take her to the potluck. When Laura picked her up, she said, "Wow, you live way out in the sticks, don't you?" Margaret's face turned red, and she once again felt different. Laura laughed and said that the ride was pretty.

When they arrived at Laura's friend's house in the city, Margaret immediately noticed that there were no men in the house. "These are all lesbians," she thought, "and they will think I am one too." Laura began introducing Margaret to the women. Then she told Margaret she was going to help in the kitchen and she was on her own. "I tell you, I just panicked when Laura left me," she told the group. A small group of women drew her into their conversation about their plans for the rest of the weekend. One woman said she was going to a gay bar on Saturday night. Another woman said she couldn't do the "bar scene" anymore and preferred to socialize at friends' homes. Then Margaret felt all eyes on her. Margaret said that she and her husband were taking the kids over to her husband's family's house. She imagined the women throwing her out of the house right then and there. What happened next surprised her. The other woman in the small group who hadn't spoken yet said that she and her boyfriend were going to see a movie that they had wanted to see for weeks. Boyfriend? Did she hear right? Maybe she just meant a boy who was a friend?

Later, Margaret was able to catch the "boyfriend woman" alone. Margaret asked Patty if she meant a friend who was a boy or a boyfriend. Patty said she meant "boyfriend," as in "you know, lover, significant other. Why do you ask?" Margaret told her that she had just assumed that all the women at the potluck except for her would be lesbians since Laura was a lesbian. Patty laughed and said that gay people don't have just other gay people as friends. "I felt a little stupid right then," she confided to the group. Margaret told Patty that she was glad she wasn't the only heterosexual and that she was glad Patty was heterosexual too. "Well, that's where you are wrong in your assumptions, girlfriend. I'm bisexual." Margaret said to Patty, "You mean you like men and women?" Patty told Margaret that during her first relationship with a woman, she had tried to convince herself and the woman that she was a lesbian. However, her attraction toward men never went away even though she loved this woman. After they broke up, Patty's friends, many of whom she had met when she was with her first female lover, encouraged her to date other women. Patty had been friends with a guy named Roland for a long time. He had also just been through a recent breakup. Patty and Roland found themselves spending more and more time together and soon they became romantically involved. "It hasn't always been easy," Patty noted, "with my gay friends wondering why I'm with a man and the fact that we are in an interracial relationship—I'm Asian and Roland is African American. Also he's ten years older than I am—I'm 25 and he's 35." Margaret asked Patty why she considered herself bisexual if she was with a man now. Patty told her it was because she still had feelings of same-sex attraction toward women that she didn't want to deny; however, she was in a committed relationship with a man, and she wouldn't act on those feelings while in the relationship.

Margaret had a lot going through her mind on the ride home. When Laura inquired about her silence, Margaret decided to take a chance. "I'm thinking about my sheltered life and what would have happened if I met some of these people and read about gay stuff when I was younger." Laura asked Margaret if she thought she might be gay. "No, darlin', not gay, because I like men too much. But I wonder whether I might like both men and women." Laura responded, "I want you to come to this group with me that meets on Thursday nights at the Gay and Lesbian Community Center. The women who run the group are real nice, and the women who come to the group, some are gay and have been for a long time, some are bi like Patty, some are trans, and some are, well, like you, just wondering or questioning. Think it over and let me know." She told the group members, "That's how I came to know about this group, from Laura."

Two months later, Margaret decided to try out the group. She was nervous when she walked through the door, and she still is, every time she comes. Margaret is committed to Chuck and the children, and she does not want to leave that relationship. She tries to reassure Chuck that she isn't interested in leaving him, she just wants to get to know herself better and the group offers her a place to do this.

Margaret looked at her watch and said, "I've talked y'all's ears off! Why didn't someone stop me!" The facilitators and the group members assured Margaret that she did not "talk their ears off" and thanked her for her bravery in telling her story.

CORRESPONDING TEXTBOOK CHAPTERS

Chapter 4: Gay, lesbian, and bisexual identity development, by D. F. Morrow.
Chapter 6: Coming out as gay, lesbian, bisexual, and transgender, by D. F. Morrow.

ADDITIONAL READINGS

Bornstein, K. (1994). *Gender outlaw*. New York: Taylor and Francis/Routledge.

Bradford, J., Ryan, C., & Rothblum, E. D. (1994). National lesbian health care survey: Implications for mental health care. *Journal of Consulting and Clinical Psychology, 62*(2), 228–242.

Cass, V. C. (1979). Homosexual identity formation: A theoretical model. *Journal of Homosexuality, 4*(3), 219–235.

Chan, C. S. (1989). Issues of identity development among Asian-American lesbians and gay men. *Journal of Counseling and Development, 68*(1), 16–20.

Cramer, E. P., & Eldridge, T. L. (1997). Les Ms.: Creating an education and support group for lesbians. *Journal of Gay and Lesbian Social Services, 7*(1), 49–72.

Cramer, E. P., & Gilson, S. F. (1999). Queers and crips: Parallel identity development processes for persons with nonvisible disabilities and lesbian, gay, and bisexual persons. *Journal of Gay, Lesbian, and Bisexual Identity, 4*(1), 23–37.

Esterberg, K. C. (1997). *Lesbian and bisexual identities: Constructing communities, constructing selves*. Philadelphia: Temple University Press.

Rust, P. C. (1993). "Coming out" in the age of social constructionism: Sexual identity formation among lesbian and bisexual women. *Gender and Society, 7*(1), 50–77.

Sears, J. T. (1991). *Growing up gay in the South: Race, gender, and journeys of the spirit*. New York: Harrington Park Press.

Sophie, J. (1985/1986). A critical examination of stage theories of lesbian identity development. *Journal of Homosexuality, 12*(2), 38–51.

Tucker, N. (Ed.). (1995). *Bisexual politics: Theories, queries, and visions*. New York: Harrington Park Press.

Walters, K. L. (1997). Urban lesbian and gay male American Indian identity: Implications for mental health service delivery. *Journal of Gay and Lesbian Social Services, 6*(2), 43–65.

Walters, K. L., & Simoni, J. M. (1993). Lesbian and gay male group identity attitudes and self-esteem: Implications for counseling. *Journal of Counseling Psychology, 40*(1), 94–99.

QUESTIONS FOR DISCUSSION

1. An essentialist perspective of sexual orientation is that sexual identity is genetic, inborn or fixed. A person arrives at one's "true" sexual orientation by passing through and successfully mastering stages, including first awareness of same-sex attraction, testing or exploring same-sex feelings, and culminating in acceptance of one's true identity and integration with other aspects of oneself (Cass 1979; Sophie 1985/86). A social constructionist perspective does not presume that there are fixed stages of identity development. Rather, sexual orientation is a social construct. One's sexual identity is dynamic and is influenced by social, cultural, and political contexts (Esterberg 1997; Rust 1993). LaTonya told the group "God blessed me by making me black and making me gay." Would you characterize LaTonya's perspective on sexual orientation as being essentialist or social constructionist? Why?

2. Through what stages did LaTonya pass in her process of lesbian identity development?

3. When she begins to tell her story, Margaret comments, "I wasn't as sure as you, LaTonya, and I'm still not." What pressures might Margaret have felt in her life to "be sure" about her sexual orientation? How might the contexts of Margaret's upbringing, her rural community, and her values and expectations about marriage and children influence her exploration of her sexual orientation? Likewise, how might the contexts of an academic community, a women's studies course, and exposure to lesbian, bisexual, and trans women influence her exploration of her sexual orientation?

4. How was Patty, the woman Margaret met at the potluck, able to work through her feelings of same-sex and opposite-sex attraction?

5. In what ways could a support group be helpful for women who are processing issues related to sexual orientation?

EXERCISE

Name: The Support Group

Purpose: To provide an in-class simulation of a support group for lesbian, bisexual, trans, and questioning women. The simulation will allow the material in the case study to "come alive" and offer an opportunity for some students to practice group facilitation skills and for other students to take on the role of group member.

Structure: The class will engage in a simulated group session based on the case study. Six to eight students will be asked to volunteer for facilitator or member roles in the group. Each volunteer will receive an index card with a brief description of a person in group and her issues related to sexual identity development. After the simulated group, the class will discuss the content of the group discussion, the process of the group, and the strengths and limitations of the work of the facilitators.

Implementation: (a) The case study for required reading will be assigned before class meets. (b) On the basis of the case study material, the class will role-play a group session on the topic of sharing coming out stories. (c) The instructor will ask for six to eight students to volunteer for facilitator and member roles. (d) Each volunteer receives an index card (see below) and is given time to read the card and mentally prepare for the role. (e) The role-play volunteers will arrange their chairs in a circle or semicircle in front of the rest of the class. (f) The instructor asks the facilitators (or facilitator if only one facilitator is desired) to begin the group. (g) Enough time is allowed for some content issues and process issues to develop (typically 15–25 minutes) and then the role-play session ends. (h) The instructor asks each volunteer how he/she felt in the role and requests feedback about the content, process, and facilitation of the group from the rest of the class.

Suggested Social Work Courses: This exercise would likely be appropriate for undergraduate and graduate direct practice courses, particularly those covering group methods. Additionally, the exercise could be modified for human behavior and social environment courses, with a focus more on the identity development issues that the volunteer group members discussed during the role-play exercise rather than the content, process, and facilitation of the group. Courses on practice with lesbians, gays, bisexuals, and transgender people and/or courses on cultural diversity/oppressed groups would also be appropriate venues for this exercise.

Suggested Class Size: The role-playing would require 6–8 students; therefore, a minimum class size of 12 would be ideal, thereby allowing for some observers and participants.

Materials and Time: The classroom should have enough space to rearrange chairs so that a simulated group session can occur and the rest of the class can easily observe. The instructor will need to prepare index cards for the volunteer roles. The whole exercise takes 35–60 minutes, depending on how long the instructor allows the role-playing to go on and how much time is spent in processing the result.

21

HOMELESS BECAUSE I AM DIFFERENT! HOMELESS YOUTH: STORIES FROM THE FIELD

Donna McIntosh

BACKGROUND INFORMATION

The U.S. Department of Health and Human Services, as part of the Juvenile Justice and Delinquency Prevention Act of 1974, provides funding for more than three hundred emergency shelters for runaway and homeless youths. Youths in crisis can stay in federally funded emergency shelters for up to two weeks while shelter staff work either to reunite them with their families, when possible, or to find safe, longer-term living arrangements when home is not an option (Family and Youth Services Bureau, 2004).

JASON'S STORY

Jason, a tall and slender white adolescent male, appeared late in the night at the shelter door asking for a place to stay. During the intake assessment, Jason disclosed that he had been out of his home for the last three months. He had been "living here and there and around" since being told to leave his family home. At that point, that was all he was willing to share. Staff offered Jason a quick meal and assigned him a bed for the night. The next day, with the counselor, Jason disclosed more of his story. He said he was 15 (he had originally told the intake worker he was 17). He also had been out of his home closer to six months than three and had been living with various friends during that time. He said that the last place he was staying "got weird" and he had to leave. Jason had made three attempts to return home by contacting his mother, but each time she hung up on him. During the next few days, more of Jason's story emerged. When the counselor approached him with the possibility of a family counseling session, Jason said, "Don't bother. Unless I go straight, I ain't welcome at home." With some prompting, he told the counselor his parents had found out he was gay. How they found out he didn't know, because he hadn't told them. The big blowup with his family ended with him on the street with only the clothes he was wearing. He tried to sneak back into the house once for his belongings, only to be caught by his father, who "beat him up." His father told him that if he ever set foot on the property again, he would be arrested—or worse!

Over the course of his stay, staff attempted to involve Jason's school social worker and child protective services workers in developing a longer-term housing option for him. It appeared at that time that neither Jason nor his family were willing to reconcile. Contact with his maternal grandmother in a neighboring state resulted in her agreeing to take Jason into her home, providing he didn't bring "his lifestyle" home with him. "After all," she told staff, "he's just a kid. What does he know about what he is and isn't?" Nine days after arriving at the shelter, Jason was on a bus to his grandmother's house.

As often happens with runaway and homeless youth, living arrangements may not be stable for very long. Over the next three years, Jason reentered the shelter approximately six times. As he got older, the homes of family and friends ran out as an option for him. He was coming back to the shelter more frequently and staying longer. It became obvious to staff that Jason was also prostituting himself for a place to stay and something to eat. He became increasingly open with staff and shelter residents about these sexual encounters and his popularity on the streets. He rationalized the encounters by saying, "At least someone loves me." During his last stay, shelter staff determined that he had engaged in sexual contact with another resident.

Jason did not deny the sexual contact. Although he complied with privilege restrictions for his and other residents' safety after the confrontation with staff about his in-shelter sexual behavior, he became increasingly unwilling to live within the guidelines of the shelter. The staff were dismayed. They had seen this pattern with other youths who had been on the street too long. Jason was now so street-wise and street-involved, it had become difficult for him to live in the shelter setting, and this situation had developed despite the now long-term relationships that he had with many of the staff members, who had come to know him well and to care deeply about him.

Once Jason turned 18, he could no longer be housed at the shelter. However, he remained in contact with several staff members. He would show up looking for a place to shower, food to eat, or help with housing or other referrals.

The last call about Jason came from one of his friends, who informed the staff that Jason had been found dead in his bed from an apparent alcohol/drug overdose.

PETER'S STORY

Peter's story involved a complicated family situation. His mother abandoned him when he was a baby and returned to her native Caribbean island community. As a result, Peter was raised by his maternal grandparents. He was 17 when he came to the shelter. He and his grandfather had exchanged blows and Peter ran. Peter wanted nothing to do with returning to his grandparents' home. He acknowledged that he loved his grandmother but said his grandfather was "one mean man." His grandmother called the shelter repeatedly to beg Peter to come home. He would talk to her briefly, but as soon as she started to make excuses for his grandfather's behavior, he would hang up on her.

As the staff learned, Peter had been physically disciplined by his grandfather all his life. As they both got older, the disciplinary encounters grew increasingly violent. The last time, the grandfather had hit Peter with a belt across the back and legs. Shelter staff took pictures of the welts and cuts and filed a child abuse report. Child protective services workers interviewed Peter and his grandparents. Peter told them he wasn't going home. His grandfather said he could come home anytime he wanted to watch his smart mouth, be respectful, and stop acting like a "faggot." His grandparents agreed that the last battle between Peter and his grandfather had gotten out of hand. The grandparents were sure it wouldn't happen again if Peter stopped acting and talking so queer. His grandmother thought Peter acted that way because he knew it irritated his grandfather. Child protective services workers saw no reason why Peter shouldn't return home, so long as Peter and his grandparents entered counseling with either the shelter counselor, the school social worker, or another counselor. Peter refused. He said, "I've had enough of that old man."

A week into Peter's stay at the shelter, a woman called the shelter and wanted to meet with Peter and his counselor. When questioned about the call, Peter disclosed that this woman was his mother and that in the last two months she had been coming around, acting like his best friend. He told staff he didn't even know her and he was really mad at her for leaving him with his grandfather. Peter also said that his mother was introducing him to her "lesbo friends." He said, "I finally figured out why I am gay—thanks to my mother."

Counseling sessions with Peter and his mother clearly displayed that both of them struggled with issues of past abandonment, sexual orientation, and identity, as well as role confusion between parent and child. It became increasingly apparent that Peter was having a hard time handling all of this at the same time. He started to verbally berate staff and other residents. When he wasn't yelling at others, he became increasingly withdrawn and isolated. Staff, in a team meeting, felt a mental health evaluation might be in order, as Peter's stress level seemed to be escalating. When the shelter counselor approached Peter about the mental health evaluation, his response was, "Fine! Now I'm crazy as well as gay!"

The next day Peter went to school, but he didn't return to the shelter. The shelter counselor was notified late that night by a social worker at the local hospital that Peter had been found lying in the middle of the road in town and had a dangerously high level of alcohol in his bloodstream. Other residents disclosed that they had seen Peter going to a bar in town where older men bought drinks for young men and gave them money and other stuff.

Peter was admitted to the hospital and, upon discharge, he went to live with his mother. After that, shelter staff saw Peter around town on occasion. Once he called and talked to staff to apologize for taking his anger out on them and other kids in the shelter. Peter said that he and his mother had worked through a lot of their problems and were actually doing pretty well. They had been going to counseling regularly and were working at living together as parent and child. He was finishing his last year of high school and thinking about college in the fall.

JAIME'S STORY

At intake, Jaime, age 17, disclosed that she was, in fact, male, but she had been dressing and passing herself off as female for the last three years. Jaime told staff she wanted "THE operation," as she described it, but it was too expensive. So she just had to settle for dressing like a girl. Immediately staff knew they had a problem. In the shelter building, boys were housed on the second floor and girls on the third. Where to put Jaime? And what about shower time? And what about managing the other teens in residence?

The staff members on duty called a meeting while Jaime was eating lunch. After a short discussion, it was decided that Jaime would stay in the single-bed room on the girls' floor and would be assigned a separate, private shower time. Staff were to address Jaime as female, since she had indicated that this was her preference. Shift staff expressed concern about the other residents and Jaime's safety from potential discrimination by them. The shelter director worried about staff and their acceptance of Jaime.

Shelter policies prohibited staff from talking about one resident's life with other residents. However, group living issues, which affect all residents, could be discussed at the weekly group residence meeting. Right away, some of the other shelter residents starting calling Jaime names and warning her to stay away from them. Jaime's response to other residents seemed to be to shock them or get in their faces. Jaime's latest response was to carry a purse and at one point pull out a tampon and declare, "It's that time of month! And good thing, because I just had an abortion a while back."

At the weekly case conference, Jaime's needs were reviewed by all shelter staff. During the meeting, a plan was developed to challenge residents about their discriminatory behavior, as well as to reinforce the policy that everyone in residence is responsible for a safe shelter. Staff noted that Jaime was not only physically a male who dressed and presented as a female but also the only African American in the shelter at that time. Race and sexual orientation seemed to be two areas in which prejudices were evident, being perpetrated in bold ways by residents and perhaps in more subtle ways by some staff members. At the end of the case conference meeting, the shelter director asked staff to remain and spent some time encouraging them to address their own reactions and concerns to Jaime's presence in the shelter. It became clear that the staff wanted to help Jaime, but they needed more guidance and training to assist Jaime and other youths who were likely to come to the shelter with similar needs.

CORRESPONDING TEXTBOOK CHAPTERS

Chapter 5: Transgender identity, by J. I. Martin & D. R. Yonkin
Chapter 6: Coming out as gay, lesbian, bisexual, and transgender, by D. F. Morrow
Chapter 8: Gay, lesbian, bisexual, and transgender adolescents, by D. F. Morrow

ADDITIONAL READING

Family and Youth Services Bureau.(2004, March). *Family and Youth Services Bureau—Basic Center Program.* Retrieved June 9, 2004, from Administration for Children and Families Online Reports, http://www.acf.dhhs.gov/programs/fysb/basic.htm.
Powers, J., Eckenrode, J., & Jaklitsch, B. (1990). Maltreatment among runaway and homeless youth. *Child Abuse and Neglect, 14*(1), 87–93.

QUESTIONS FOR DISCUSSION

1. What did the three cases have in common? What was unique about each case?

2. At what stage of sexual identity and "coming out" was each of these youths at the time he or she entered the shelter and how did that affect plans to return home or to find a safe alternative?

3. What types of intake questions and service planning might you as a shelter case manager incorporate to better serve these youths?

4. How might shelters deal with balancing individual privacy with group living concerns and issues? Were there instances in these cases where group living safety might have taken precedence over continued sheltering of the individual?

5. What organizational and community factors (i.e., resources, policies, institutional discrimination, and so on) were present in these cases, or might be present in such cases, that the shelter should address to better serve these youths?

6. How might a statewide advocacy coalition for runaway and homeless youths, which provides training and technical assistance, be of assistance to emergency shelters serving gay/lesbian/bisexual/transgender and questioning youths? How might such a coalition work to advocate for this subpopulation among runaway and homeless youths in this country?

EXERCISES

EXERCISE 1

Name: Working with GLBT and Questioning Youth in Emergency Shelters

Purpose: To utilize micro, mezzo, and macro practice skills to effectively develop a sensitive and responsive individual service plan for an individual client; to create and maintain a safe, respectful shelter program atmosphere among residents and between staff and residents; to address community resources and institutional discrimination

Structure: This exercise is intended to give students an opportunity to design a case plan for a homeless GLBT youth.

Implementation: The week before students participate in this exercise, it is suggested that students and the instructor go online at the Department of Human Services to gather background information about emergency shelters for runaway or homeless youths. Another option is to have a guest speaker come from an area shelter to talk about shelter services and how they might address such cases in their shelter programs. Many communities have emergency shelters within a day's travel.

After students have gained the appropriate background information, the class will be divided into four groups. Each of the groups will be assigned one of the cases and instructed to role-play one of the following scenarios:

a. A case conference with shelter staff and the youth to determine a service plan that also addresses the youth's sexual identity needs. Shelter staff identified for the exercise might include case manager, intake worker, director, youth workers, house manager, counselor, activities director.

b. A family counseling session

c. A meeting of shelter staff with community service providers, including child protective services, school social worker, family, and youth to determine where the youth is going to live

d. A shelter staff meeting that puts forth staff concerns about managing sexual orientation needs and sexual activity among youths in shelter residence

After each of the role-plays has been performed, the audience will provide feedback and suggestions on the exercise.

EXERCISE 2

Name: Advocating for GLBT and Questioning Youths at the Macro Level

Purpose: To use a case as a tool for advocating at the state and national levels for the needs of runaway and homeless youths, particularly the unique needs of the GLBT population of homeless youths

Structure: This exercise is intended to help students design a state or national policy advocacy activity (examples might be poster campaigns, legislative testimony, a public education campaign, a speak-out, a shelter brochure and other public relations materials such as media ads that highlight the needs of this population) that would promote public awareness and sensitivity to street youths or build support from state or national legislators for funding of programs that serve this population.

Implementation: Within the classroom, students may work for part or all of a semester in teams on different policy advocacy activities aimed at promoting public sensitivity to this population or at increasing fiscal support from legislators. This activity may be constructed as a "simulation" of what students would do to achieve such policy objectives. The instructor may also link the students to a statewide, regional, or national coalition for runaway and homeless youths in an effort to complete an actual policy project that would be designed and implemented in a partnership between students and the advocacy organization.

Suggested Social Work Courses: Human behavior and the social environment; child welfare; practice

Suggested Class Size: 20–30 students

Materials and Time: No specific materials are required. The ideal time for a role-play is a one-hour class period, with the following one-hour class used for processing the experience.

22

GENDER IDENTITY CASE HISTORIES

D. R. Yonkin

THE GAY, lesbian, bisexual, and transgender community center offers several support groups for people who want to explore their gender identity in various ways. A group called TransQueer and Questioning assists those individuals who identify as "gender different" or "queer" in some way, as well as those who are just beginning to seek guidance and support for newly emerging gender identity issues. TQ&Q is the oldest of all the trans groups, and it still maintains an informal, drop-in approach. It is co-facilitated by a skilled social worker and a graduate student intern, who together can assess and refer clients to appropriate formal groups and other relevant services offered by the center. Both workers are supervised by the center's mental health clinical director. The following three cases represent clients who came to the GLBT center and were recommended for the TransQueer and Questioning group as the best place to start.

EDDIE'S STORY

Eddie arrives half an hour early for TQ&Q and waits nervously for others to show up. He is wearing dirty jeans and a long-sleeved shirt despite the July heat and humidity. Although he is 25, he appears much younger and his voice breaks like that of a young teenage boy. He has medium-length, unwashed hair and a very light but obvious mustache.

Eddie introduces himself to the group as someone who is "confused," adding that he had once attended a different support group there but left because of a "bad experience." He has worked for a year in a coffee shop and describes himself as "an agnostic Jew." He says that his parents, now in their sixties, are both children of Dutch Holocaust survivors. He describes growing up as "miserable from day one" and says that his parents "continuously antagonized" him since birth. He moved out a year ago after what began as a typical violent argument with his parents. However, this time his mother screamed, *"Flikker!* [queer!]—you should never have lived! We should never have let them make you a *niese* [girl] and given you away instead!" With an obvious mixture of revulsion and relief, they told him the following story:

When he was born the doctor had told them in hushed and pitying tones that there was "a birth defect." The baby would never be able to have normal sexual relations or children of its own. He awkwardly explained that although the baby had "sex parts," it was neither a boy nor a girl. For the sake of the child there was no other option but to accept the doctor's medical opinion and do exactly what he recommended. Unfortunately, the hospital could not "fix it" and the only recourse was to raise the child as female. Confused and frightened, the parents agreed to this, as well as to the doctor's repeated directive to never disclose the truth to the child or to anyone else. The baby was named Edda after the father's grandmother, and he was dressed and socialized as a girl from that day on.

Now, sitting in the group, Eddie recalls his childhood as a girl. Made wary of others, "Edda" was isolated as a child, spending all her free time in the library as soon as she could go there by herself. At age 15, she found books that seemed to indicate she might be a lesbian. However, feeling that she was the only one around, she became further isolated. At age 18, she found a flyer for a lesbian support group at the gay and lesbian center and went to a meeting. For some reason, she did not feel as if she belonged there—nor did the other women seem to be comfortable around her. One young woman said Edda was too "butch," a term she didn't understand. Another angrily accused her of being "some kind of guy in disguise." Feeling hurt and threatened, Edda fled the group. This is Eddie's first time back to the center since he discovered and claimed his male identity.

GREGORIO'S STORY

Gregorio, a 39-year-old Latino, is unemployed and lives alone just outside the city where the GLBT center is located. He has explored the S&M scene in bars and clubs in the city since he was 19 and prefers to wear women's clothing while engaging in sex. He labels himself "bisexual." He has met several transwomen at the clubs, finding them "interesting" and "often attractive." Gregorio's preference for female clothing has recently increased, and he has begun having fantasies about having a female body with breasts. Although these fantasies give him sexual pleasure, he feels guilty about them, as well as about his occasional thoughts to explore further by taking female hormones.

He takes an antidepressant prescribed by a psychiatrist because he was experiencing an increasing lack of motivation and was sleeping fourteen hours or more every day. He brought his fantasy concerns to his psychiatrist, who scanned through the *DSM-IV-TR* and informed Gregorio that she diagnosed him with transvestic fetishism and gender identity disorder. The psychiatrist, who did not feel competent to work with these issues, advised Gregorio to seek counseling at the GLBT center in the city. Gregorio did not want to see a therapist at that time. Yet he recently had a depressive episode and became frightened by thoughts of taking an overdose of his prescription. He called the GLBT center the next day and the intake worker suggested that he attend the TransQueer and Questioning group, which was meeting that night. He changed his mind about asking about a therapist because he was afraid to disclose his suicidal ideation.

Dressed in spandex bike shorts and a sleeveless sweatshirt that emphasize his short, muscular frame, Gregorio gives an immediate and strong male presentation. His dark hair is in a buzz cut, and his eyebrows appear to be plucked very thin, giving an incongruous look to his otherwise very masculine face. During the initial round of introductions in the group, two of the members share that they just came from an Alcoholics Anonymous meeting. Seemingly encouraged by this, Gregorio reports that he is in recovery from alcohol abuse and attends an AA group. He also shares concerns that he might have sexual addiction issues as well. He has a computer and online access, which he uses primarily to surf for pornography and to make sexual contacts.

Just as the group is ending, the student facilitator notices what appear to be bra straps slipping from beneath Gregorio's shirt. Observing the worker's face, Gregorio asks, "Is anything wrong?"

CALVIN'S STORY

The caller's voice sounded soft but obviously male and very nervous when he called the GLBT center. He introduced himself as "Calvin" and said only that "the problem is about my sex identity." The intake clinician suggested that he try the weekly TransQueer and Questioning support group as a place to start, adding that private counseling services were also available. Calvin did not respond to the counseling suggestion, but he asked for the center's address and politely thanked the clinician for the information.

Calvin travels by bus to TQ&Q dressed as a man and then puts on a little makeup in the gender-free restroom at the center. An African American, he is well over six feet tall and presently shaves his hair very close to his head. He sometimes wears bracelets and gold earrings, and although his nails are short, they are usually painted in dark colors. Today he is wearing a skirt to the group for the first time, and his nails are a bright red.

Calvin has carefully revealed his story over a period of six TQ&Q group sessions. He reports that he was born "a healthy baby boy" but remembers feeling that he was really a girl since the age of 4. He grew up in a small Southern town, where he lived with his mother, who was a factory laborer until a back injury left her disabled. Calvin dropped out of school at 17 and the family had no source of income other than his mother's disability checks. When he was 20, they moved to their present apartment on the outskirts of a large metropolitan area in the North.

Calvin was always dressed as a boy until he insisted on wearing dresses at the age of 11, to which his mother reluctantly acceded. Although he was allowed to dress as a girl when at home, his mother insisted that he dress in male clothing and "act like a real man" outside the house. During puberty, Calvin prayed nightly for God to "please make me wake up the girl I am." At the age of 14, he discovered that sometimes smoking a little marijuana and sitting in front of a mirror "helped me relax into my true nature." Now, sensing more anonymity in his new environment, he has experimented with leaving the apartment at night dressed as a woman, but only to walk to a corner store a block away. He has never entered the store.

At the most recent TQ&Q, Calvin shared with the group that, at the age of 22, he is finally aware that he longs to be "all woman all the time." He asked in a quiet voice if the group could now call him "Cassy." He went on to report that he had found a gay bar that hosts a night for cross-dressers, and he recently made friends with a woman there who he thinks is also male-bodied. She offered him some free hormone injections, as well as opportunities to make quick money by having sex with men who frequented the bar looking for partners. Seeing the chance to "make me more of a woman," he accepted both offers.

CORRESPONDING TEXTBOOK CHAPTERS

Chapter 5: Transgender identity, by J. I. Martin & D. R. Yonkin.
Chapter 12: Transgender emergence within families, by A. I. Lev.
Chapter 15: Transgender health issues, by E. Lombardi & S. M. Davis,

ADDITIONAL READINGS

Bullough, B., & Bullough, V. (1997). Men who cross-dress: A survey. In B. Bullough, V. Bullough, & J. Elias (Eds.), *Gender blending* (pp. 174–188). Amherst, NY: Prometheus Books.

Devor, H. (1997). *FTM: Female-to-male transsexuals in society.* Indianapolis: Indiana University Press.

Docter, R. F., & Prince, V. (1997). Transvestism: A survey of 1032 cross-dressers. *Archives of Sexual Behavior,* 26(6), 589–605.

Dreger, A. D. (1998). *Hermaphrodites and the medical invention of sex.* Cambridge, MA: Harvard University Press.

——. (1999). *Intersex in the age of ethics.* Hagerstown, MD: University Publishing Group.

Ettner, R. (1999). *Gender loving care: A guide to counseling gender-variant clients.* New York: Norton.

Intersex Society of North America. (2002). *ISNA's recommendations for treatment.* Retrieved April 26, 2005, from http://www.isna.org/library/recommendations.html.

Kessler, S. J. (2000). *Lessons from the intersexed.* New Brunswick, NJ: Rutgers University Press.

Kirk, S. (1996a). *Feminizing hormonal therapy for the transgendered.* Blawnox, PA: Together Lifeworks.

——. (1996b). *Masculinizing hormonal therapy for the transgendered.* Blawnox, PA: Together Lifeworks.

Leslie, D. R., Perina, B. A., & Maqueda, M. C. (2001). Clinical issues with transgender individuals. In *A provider's introduction to substance abuse treatment for lesbian, gay, bisexual, and transgender individuals* (pp. 91–98). Retrieved April 26, 2005, from http://media.shs.net/prevline/pdfs/BKD392/index.pdf.

Lev, A. I. (2004). *Transgender emergence: Therapeutic guidelines for working with gender-variant people and their families.* New York: Haworth Clinical Practice Press.

National Institute on Drug Abuse. (2002). *Research report: Steroid abuse and addiction.* NIH Publication no. 00–3721. Retrieved April 26, 2005, from www.nida.nih.gov/ResearchReports/Steroids/anabolicsteroids3.html.

QUESTIONS FOR DISCUSSION

1. What kind of training should the TQ&Q group facilitators have?

2. What kinds of personal or professional issues might arise for you in running this kind of group?

3. What kinds of policies and procedures should the TQ&Q group have in place to help all people attending to feel comfortable and safe?

4. Are there any problems that you could foresee arising in a group that contained all three of these people? How might you proactively address these problems?

5. Regarding Gregorio's case, how could the student intern respond to his question?

EXERCISE

Name: Team Assessment

Structure: The exercise employs a teamwork approach. The questions below are used to help identify and frame a client's salient core issue or issues, sub-issues, and how the issues are related to one another.

Implementation: The class is divided into several teams of equal number, and each team is assigned a different case and a group spokesperson. Students will discuss as many of the following questions as possible, while the teacher visits each group to listen and guide as needed. The class reconvenes after 15 minutes.

1. What, if any, are the gender issues that the client reports or appears to have?
2. How should the client be addressed when spoken to?
3. How should the client be referred to when discussing the case with others?
4. What are the client's strengths and challenges?
5. What are any risks the client faces?
6. What roles do significant others play in the client's life?
7. What are the salient issues of the case?
8. In what order of importance should the needs of the client be prioritized?
9. Is the client in the right place at this time?
10. What feelings does the client bring up for you?

When the class reassembles, each group's spokesperson will read the group's case to the class and report their assessments and referrals (30–45 minutes). The teacher can list salient features and problems of the case on the blackboard. The teacher might conduct an open class discussion about how a team approach is useful (or not) for these cases, as well as other issues or questions that appear significant in any of them.

Suggested Social Work Courses: Practice classes

Suggested Class Size: 15–18 students

Materials and Time: The materials needed are a blackboard and chalk, and paper and pen for notes. This exercise will take about 80 minutes.

PART 4

ORGANIZATIONS AND COMMUNITIES

THE FOUR chapters in this section address agency policy development and revision (chapters 23 and 24) and community organizing (chapters 25 and 26). Chapter 23 describes the impact of (a lack of) organizational policy on GLBT employees in a human service organization. Chapter 24 raises the issue of how agency policies can be changed to keep them in line with local and state policies and to advocate for the rights of GLBT people. In each case, social workers are seen as central change agents in organizational settings, even if their official job entails more direct practice. In this way, even more clinically oriented students can use these cases to consider how, why, and at what cost they might engage in macro-level activities to improve policies within organizations for GLBT staff and clients.

In chapter 25, students are presented with the intersecting paths of different actors (friends, parents, advocates, service providers) in a social movement to recognize domestic violence in same-sex and transgender relationships. Students begin to see how these actors could come together as a coalition to raise awareness, improve services to GLBT victims and their families, and work to prevent future violence in these relationships. In chapter 26, students learn about the role of religious leaders (and religious arguments) in community organizing around social policies. These cases, which are located in the American South, can also raise for students the issue of regional similarities and differences as they relate to community organizing.

23

"BUILDING EXCUSES" IN THE WORKPLACE

Kristina M. Hash

ELIZABETH IS a 50-year-old African American female. She is employed as a nurse at a large, for-profit nursing home facility in a small community in the southeastern United States. She has been with the organization for almost ten years and is considered compassionate and reliable by the nursing home staff. Although she appears to be single, it is rumored among the facility that her "roommate" and she "are queer together."

In the past few months she has called in sick on several occasions and has used the majority of her vacation leave. Lately, she also appears exhausted and stressed on the job. Jane, a social worker in the nursing home, approaches Elizabeth and mentions her concern that she appears very stressed and asks if there is anything she would like to talk about. Elizabeth reveals that she is dealing with a very difficult personal situation, specifically that her partner of fifteen years, Teresa, is experiencing serious health problems. These problems have required that Elizabeth travel with Teresa to several medical appointments and provide hands-on care at home.

Although Teresa's mother and sister have been helping out, they are not comfortable with the same-sex relationship and their interactions are often strained. Elizabeth shares her concern with the social worker that she is the "sole breadwinner" of the household and does not want to risk losing her job by taking so much time off. She is tired of hiding the situation and of "burning up" all of her vacation time. She also feels drained from having to "build excuses" for why she must take time off, such as "I have personal business to take care of" or "My best friend is ill and her mother needs someone to help take care of her."

In a recent meeting, the staff reviewed staff benefits, including family leave and spousal medical insurance. Elizabeth says that she had a hard time to keep from crying because she knew this benefit did not apply to her situation. She shares with the social worker her inclination to explain her difficult circumstances to her other coworkers and the administration, but she fears that her relationship will not be accepted and her situation will not be supported.

CORRESPONDING TEXTBOOK CHAPTERS

Chapter 10: Lesbian relationships and families, by C. A. Parks & N. A. Humphreys.
Chapter 18: Workplace issues, by K. M. Hash.

ADDITIONAL READINGS

Badgett, M. V. L. (1996). Employment and sexual orientation: Disclosure and discrimination in the workplace. *Journal of Gay and Lesbian Social Services, 4*(4), 29–52.

Besner, H. F., & Spungin, C. I. (1998). *Training for professionals who work with gays and lesbians in educational and workplace settings*. Washington, DC: Accelerated Development.

Human Rights Campaign. (2001). *The state of the workplace for lesbian, gay, bisexual, and transgender Americans in 2001*. Washington, DC: Human Rights Campaign Foundation.

McNaught, B. (1995). *Gay issues in the workplace*. New York: St. Martin's.

Powers, B., & Ellis, A. (1995). *A manager's guide to sexual orientation in the workplace*. New York: Routledge.

Sussal, C. M. (1994). Empowering gays and lesbians in the workplace. *Journal of Gay and Lesbian Social Services, 1*(1), 89–103.

Winfeld, L., & Spielman, S. (2001). *Straight talk about gays in the workplace* (2nd ed.). New York: Harrington Park Press.

Zuckerman, A. J., & Simons, G. (1996). *Sexual orientation in the workplace: Gay men, lesbians, bisexuals, and heterosexuals working together*. Thousand Oaks, CA: Sage.

QUESTIONS FOR DISCUSSION

1. What are the special issues faced by Elizabeth and members of this population in society and in the workplace?

2. If Elizabeth decides to come out at work, what are some of the negative attitudes and behaviors that may surface among coworkers or the administration?

3. How should negative attitudes and behaviors be handled or prevented? By whom should they be handled?

4. How can the agency and its staff support Elizabeth as well as other GLBT employees?

5. What is the "state of the workplace" in your state and local community? (For policies regarding GLBT employees, see the Human Rights Campaign Web site and/or the document *The state of the workplace for lesbian, gay, bisexual, and transgender Americans*, at www.hrc.org). What are the policies regarding GLBT employees at your university? Place of employment? Field agency?*

6. What can be done in the larger community and at the state and national levels to support Elizabeth and other GLBT employees? What can be done in your university, place of employment, or field agency?*

*Questions 5 and 6 may require that the facilitator and participants do some preparatory work before class meets.

EXERCISE

Name: Organizational Change Role-Play

Purpose: To sensitize participants to the special issues faced by GLBT people in the workplace and engage them in problem-solving strategies related to these issues

Structure: This exercise is a group activity using role-play and discussion. It can be accomplished within a regular classroom or workshop setting.

Implementation: Participants are divided into four groups of five or more. Each group is to read the case described above. Each group member will role-play one of the following individuals:

- Elizabeth (the lesbian employee), who wants partner benefits
- The administrator(s), who want(s) to save money, serve clients, maintain stable organizational structure, maintain community support, maintain stable staffing
- Agency social worker(s), who want(s) to get partner benefits in order to enhance equity among workers
- Other coworker(s), who are not committed to partner benefits and may have various perspectives and concerns
- Human resources personnel, who want to clarify the benefits package, will be responsible for implementing any decision, may have various perspectives and concerns

Each group member will represent his/her role in a staff meeting called to finalize a benefits package for employees. The package includes health insurance, a medical savings account, and family leave policies. An agency social worker will bring up his/her concern that the package is not sensitive to the needs of GLBT staff. It is anticipated that some of the staff in attendance will not be in favor of policies supporting GLBT employees. At the conclusion of the role-play, groups will report the major points of their discussion to the larger class/workshop.

Suggested Class Size: 10 or more

Materials and Time: Descriptions of the roles and the case description. The exercise will last 30–45 minutes.

24

DESIGNING A STRATEGY FOR CHANGING AGENCY POLICY

Nancy A. Humphreys and Cheryl A. Parks

YOU ARE a professionally trained BSW or MSW social worker at a private adoption agency in a state that has recently passed legislation guaranteeing civil rights protections to gays and lesbians. You and some of your colleagues are committed to working to change agency policy so that gay and lesbian couples can adopt openly—i.e., can openly acknowledge their sexual orientation and be considered a couple, with both individuals becoming official parents through adoption. Currently the agency understands that some "single-parent" adoptions are in fact adoptions by gay or lesbian couples. There is an unwritten/unspoken agreement to a "don't ask, don't tell" policy. Using the NASW *Code of Ethics* and the new legislation, you intend to urge the agency to fully and completely recognize the rights of gays and lesbians as couples to adopt with both parents recognized in the adoption process. While in school you enjoyed the classes in which community and organizational content was prominent, so you decide you will organize some colleagues to present and advocate for a change in agency policy.

The agency, the XYZ Child and Family Agency, is located in a large urban center of a state in the Northeast that has a long tradition of libertarian legislation to protect the rights of oppressed and vulnerable groups. The civil rights legislation for gays and lesbians that just passed is the most recent example of such laws. As has been true in the past, however, the exact nature of the protections granted to gays and lesbians is not specified in the legislation itself. Therefore the legislation is open to interpretation. For example, students at the state-supported law school, using the legislation as a precedent, have argued that the U.S. military should no longer be allowed to recruit on campus since the branches of the military discriminate against gays and lesbians, which is now illegal, given the new legislation. The outcome of this change effort is not yet known.

The XYZ agency has generally been very progressive and has tried to stay informed about innovations in child welfare and family service practices and to incorporate them into agency policies, programs, and practices. The agency is fully accredited and is often cited as a model agency. The agency has also become well informed about trends and developments in the political arena since it has become more and more dependent on public agency funds for its operating costs. Currently, more than 75% of the agency's annual budget comes from public monies. Through a variety of grants and contracts, the agency provides a number of services that would otherwise be provided by public agencies. In addition to public funding, the agency receives United Way money, charges for some services on a sliding fee schedule, and has the advantage of a very large endowment. Approximately 9% of the total agency budget comes from interest earned from the endowment. This interest income gives the agency considerable flexibility in providing services in areas not usually funded by public sources.

Agency staff total more than 100, with approximately half being social workers, although only about two thirds of the staff are professionally trained. Staff are organized into six departments: home-based services for children, school-based services for children, foster care services, adoption, family service, and residential treatment services for children and adolescents. Centralized training, research, and development departments, as well as administrative structures, support the service departments.

The agency's chief executive officer (CEO), a white woman with an MSW, is new to the agency and the state. She has been CEO for six months. She was highly recruited as a result of her service as the director of a smaller, struggling agency in a neighboring state, which she was able to turn around. The board and staff selection committee chose her for this job in part because she had many ideas for ways to strengthen the XYZ agency and move it into new service areas, especially profitable ones. In the short time she has been at the agency, she has impressed the staff with her knowledge and commitment to serving children and families. She has also intimidated some of the staff, since she is dynamic, forceful, and powerful. Some staff speculate that she might be lesbian. She is not married and never mentions a male partner, but occasionally uses "we" references when speaking about private matters, which she does only rarely. It is clear that if she is a lesbian, she is "closeted."

You work in the adoption department as a senior clinical social worker. You have been with the agency for almost ten years and have been offered promotions many times, but each time you've turned the offer down because you enjoy client contact so much. In recognition of your many skills and your preference for retaining direct client contact, the agency created a special position for you, one that enables you to continue to work directly with clients while also supervising less-experienced staff who benefit from your experience and expertise. In your current position as senior clinical social worker, you carry a large but manageable caseload, often including the more difficult cases; at the same time, you provide clinical supervision and consultation to five other adoption workers.

The director of the adoption department, your immediate superior, has been with the agency for many years and is thinking about retirement in the next few years. She has a gay son and has shared with you and a few others during informal conversations that she thinks she must have done something wrong in the way she parented her son and she wishes he was not gay. The director has generally been successful in the adoption field and is respected. Because of her professional reputation and the agency's strength, she has recently been asked by the governor to chair a committee on permanency planning for children. The stated purpose of the committee is to explore avenues to increase the number of adoptive families for the growing number of children in state subsidized foster care who are now or soon will be available for adoption.

While the agency has a somewhat informal style, and staff at all levels tend to interact with one another comfortably and fairly easily, the agency is still very clear that it is important to follow the "chain of command" when new policies are to be considered. Like all private agencies, the top of the chain of command is the agency board of directors. The XYZ agency has been well served by its board, which is made up of some of the community's most prominent and respected citizens. Over the years, the board has been successful in assisting the agency in raising funds for new programs, expanding the reputation of the agency, and keeping the agency's policies in line with the best practices in the field. Recently, as part of a strategic planning process participated in by both board and staff, agreement was reached on a new initiative to find additional ways to work more closely and cooperatively with the state providers of child and family services.

The board has demonstrated considerable confidence in the CEO and retains the enthusiasm for her skills that they had when she was first hired. The CEO takes care to see that the board is informed and involved in all major policymaking decisions for the agency, but she is equally clear that the board should not micromanage the affairs of the agency. Any major policy change, especially one that might bring some kind of public repercussions, would always be presented to the board for a decision. The board's usual way of operating is to discuss an issue at one meeting and reach a decision at the next; in the instance of very controversial decisions, the discussion period could be longer.

CORRESPONDING TEXTBOOK CHAPTERS

Chapter 3: Oppression, prejudice, and discrimination, by D. E. Elze.
Chapter 19: Social welfare policy and advocacy, by L. Messinger.

ADDITIONAL READINGS

Brager, G., & Holloway, S. (1992). Assessing prospects for organizational change: Force field analysis. *Administration in Social Work, 16*(3/4), 15–28.
Brooks, D., & Goldberg, S. (2001). Gay and lesbian adoptive and foster placements: Can they meet the needs of waiting children? *Social Work, 46*(2), 147–157.

Gustausson, N. S. (1995). "Don't ask, don't tell" and child welfare. *Social Work*, 40(6), 815–817.

Patti, R. (1974). Organizational resistance and change: The view from below. *Social Service Review*, 48(3), 367–383.

QUESTIONS FOR DISCUSSION

1. How could you go about raising the idea of allowing gays and lesbians to adopt when all other agency qualifications are met? Whom would you want to talk with first, next, and why?

2. Who holds the decision-making authority to allow gays and lesbians to be openly considered as adoptive couples? What would be the best approach to get the decision-making authority to agree?

3. What would be the biggest concerns of various decision makers in the chain of command and how would you address these concerns?

4. Identify the forces that would support the change and those that would oppose. Consider how you would mobilize the support and reduce or ignore the opposition.

EXERCISE

Name: Changing Agency Policy: Developing a Plan

Purpose: To hone students' sensitivity to, and skills in assessment of, power and authority as forces that can both impede and facilitate policy/organizational change efforts; to develop strategies by which to mobilize support and reduce opposition to change efforts

Structure: Students will be asked to design an organizational change strategy that would have the best chance of producing a policy that would allow gays and lesbians to openly adopt.

Implementation: The class is divided into groups of four or five. Students will be advised that in thinking about the planned change effort, they should be sure to consider all of the relevant stakeholders and the position that each group would take, remembering that in a group of stakeholders there is often a range of opinions and views. To assist them in this analysis, groups will conduct a force-field analysis (Brager & Holloway, 1992). Groups will discuss and agree on the first few steps they would take to introduce and try to gain approval for the idea of including gays and lesbians among couples eligible to adopt openly.

Suggested Social Work Courses: This exercise would be appropriate for courses in which GLBT content is included or organizational change is a focus; macro foundation practice classes; macro practice classes.

Suggested Class Size: Any size class would be suitable; with larger classes, students could be divided into smaller groups of 5 to 10 members.

Materials and Time: 15 minutes for the group work, 20–30 minutes for in-class discussion of the groups' plans

25

MAKING THE LINK: DOMESTIC VIOLENCE IN THE GLBT COMMUNITY

Marcie Fisher-Borne

UNDERSTANDING PARTNER VIOLENCE IN GLBT RELATIONSHIPS

Despite the fact that domestic violence is as common in GLBT relationships as it is in heterosexual relationships, the issue of GLBT partner violence is still largely "in the closet." A growing body of research suggests that one in four gay, lesbian, bisexual, and transgender (GLBT) people is battered by a partner (Barnes, 1998). Still, many domestic violence service agencies deny that domestic violence exists in the GLBT community. The reasons for this are complex. Traditionally, domestic violence agencies lack specific training or resources to provide appropriate services to GLBT survivors of domestic violence. Legally, GLBT couples and families lack formal recognition and thus face additional obstacles. In some states, such as Virginia, individuals in violent same-gender relationships are intentionally excluded from obtaining protective orders or other legal support.

Some of the difficulties in serving GLBT survivors of domestic violence are the result of conventional approaches to domestic violence work. Heterosexual battering is often understood on the basis of "traditional gender roles." Unfortunately, stereotypes founded on gender are of little use in understanding violence in GLBT relationships. Physical attributes or notions of "masculinity" or "femininity" are not accurate indicators of whether a person is a victim or a batterer in heterosexual relationships, much less in GLBT relationships. While domestic violence is often underreported regardless of sexual orientation, GLBT victims of such violence experience multiple layers of isolation and invisibility. Because of this, working with agencies in providing appropriate services to the GLBT community and increasing awareness of the issue of domestic violence within the GLBT community is of critical importance. The following case study highlights a statewide domestic violence coalition and its work in addressing domestic violence within GLBT relationships, families, and communities.

THE COALITION

The Virginia Domestic Violence Coalition (VDVC) has served as a voice against domestic violence and sexual assault for more than twenty years. The coalition acts as a network organization for domestic violence programs throughout the state by providing public policy advocacy, community education, training, and technical assistance to build the capacity of communities to better address violence. As with many organizations in the field of domestic violence prevention, the Virginia coalition is committed to addressing the root causes of violence.

Throughout its work, the coalition emphasizes the link between individual acts of violence and institutional and systemic violence. The coalition is committed to helping domestic violence agencies understand how institutional oppression and marginalization of specific groups foster violence. Since the coalition is an organization run and staffed by primarily white, middle-class women, it has found that undoing racism and classism is at times difficult but necessary work. The coalition understands that it is not enough to say, "Everyone is welcome," but that as an agency it must intentionally and actively create safe places for all women and work to change the systems and institutions that perpetuate violence.

The work on issues of racial and economic privilege over the last ten years has laid the groundwork for beginning to address homophobia and heterosexism within the organization's domestic violence prevention efforts. "We are an organization that works daily on ending violence. Homophobia is violence in our culture," the director told her staff in their first official training on GLBT partner violence. While the agency began its work on homophobia and heterosexism, organizing was happening in the community as well.

THE CONTEXT

Stacy and Linda, a lesbian couple in the coastal area of the state, have known many friends in abusive relationships who finally reached out for help and were met with insensitive agency staff and even denied legal protection. Stacy and Linda knew other GLBT people who were afraid to come forward and report abuse for fear of being "outed." Seeing this lack of support and resources, Stacy and Laura designed a Web site that offers information and resources specifically for the GLBT community.

During the same time, in a different area of Virginia, the Tyler family began speaking out about their gay son's experience with domestic violence. After years of trying to obtain a restraining order against his ex-partner, Justin Tyler was violently murdered in his home in southern Virginia. The Tyler family realized that rural counties with few resources, like theirs, needed to face the issue of GLBT violence directly. The Tylers did not want other parents to experience such heartache, and they were determined to be a voice for change in their state.

PROJECT RAINBOW

As soon as VDVC learned about these grassroots efforts, the staff and board decided they wanted to support this important work and they invited these key community members to come together. The interest and momentum of the Tylers and Stacy and Linda, combined with VDVC's commitment as an organization to dismantling heterosexism and addressing the needs of GLBT survivors, led to the creation of a state-wide education and community initiative called Project Rainbow. The first goal of Project Rainbow was to increase awareness about GLBT domestic violence. With a small grant from a local foundation, Project Rainbow began providing training sessions around the state for staff at domestic violence agencies. The training aimed to build the capacity of individuals and domestic violence organizations to provide appropriate services to the GLBT community.

While improving existing domestic violence services was critical, the Project Rainbow leadership team knew that the most important audience was the GLBT community itself. How could they raise awareness about violence within GLBT relationships? What would it take to get GLBT communities to talk openly about the reality of partner violence? And how could they build partnerships between GLBT community agencies and domestic violence prevention efforts? In order to explore these questions more deeply, Project Rainbow decided to invite key state leaders in the fields of domestic violence prevention and GLBT advocacy to convene.

In coming together, leaders in both fields identified the need to create a statewide campaign aimed at empowering individuals and building healthier relationships and families within the GLBT community. Although the specifics of the campaign were unclear, the leaders realized that it would take family members, GLBT leaders, domestic violence agencies, and strong community support to create an initiative that could offer long-term sustainability.

CORRESPONDING TEXTBOOK CHAPTERS

Chapter 14: Health concerns for lesbians, gay men, and bisexuals, by C. Ryan & E. Gruskin
Chapter 20: Toward affirmative practice, by L. Messinger

ADDITIONAL READING

Barnes, P. (1998). It's just a quarrel. *American Bar Association Journal, 84,* 24–25.

Burke, L., & Follingstad, D. R. (1999). Violence in lesbian and gay relationships: Theory, prevalence, and correlational factors. *Clinical Psychology Review, 19*(5), 487–512.

Domestic violence in gay and lesbian relationships. (2005). Retrieved on June 9, 2005, from Abuse, Rape, and Domestic Violence Aid and Resource Collection, http://www.aardvarc.org/samesex/about.shtml.

Girshick, L. B. (2002). *Woman-to-woman sexual violence: Does she call it rape?* Boston: Northeastern University Press.

National Coalition of Anti-Violence Programs. (2003). *LGBT Supplement: An Update from the national coalition of anti-violence programs.* Retrieved June 9, 2005, from the National Coalition of Anti-Violence Programs, http://www.avp.org/publications/reports/2003NCAVPdvrpt.pdf.

QUESTIONS FOR DISCUSSION

1. How does domestic violence uniquely affect GLBT people?

2. Considering these differences, how should domestic violence agency services be modified to provide support?

3. What is the significance of the Tylers' and Linda and Stacy's roles in the formation and sustainability of Project Rainbow? How would you suggest agencies work to gain grassroots support of their prevention efforts?

4. What would be the key steps in designing a statewide campaign to empower GLBT people to build healthy relationships and strong families?

EXERCISE

Name: Stakeholders Meeting

Purpose: To give students an opportunity to consider the key steps in organizing a community-based campaign involving diverse partners

Structure: Students will work in small groups to plan and role-play a "stakeholders" meeting to determine the key elements for a campaign related to GLBT domestic violence.

Implementation: This activity should be done immediately following the case study. The class will be divided into groups of six to eight students. Each group will identify the key players who should be invited to a stakeholders meeting. After the group has done this part of the exercise, the individual students in the group will choose which of these designated leaders they wish to role-play in a "Project Rainbow" meeting. In their roles, they must decide the following and record their decisions:

1. What kind of initiative will you create? Why?
2. Will it be local, regional, or statewide?
3. What are the major goals of your initiative? How will you know they are met?
4. What is the time line?
5. How will you sustain your initiative over time?

After 20–30 minutes of small-group discussion, all groups will report back to the entire class.

Suggested Social Work Courses: Community practice; social work policy

Suggested Class Size: 20–30 students

Materials and Time: This activity relies on students' knowledge of the case study. Newsprint and markers will be needed for the small-group stakeholder meetings. Small-group discussions will take 20–30 minutes, and the small groups' reports to the entire class will each take 5 minutes. The discussion will take 45–75 minutes, depending on class size.

26

A LEAP OF FAITH: SOUTHERN MINISTERS ORGANIZING FOR CHANGE

Marcie Fisher-Borne .

THE YEAR 2004 marked a new era in the struggle for equality and justice for the GLBT community. While marriages between same-sex couples became legal in Massachusetts, "Defense of Marriage" amendments codified discrimination against same-sex couples as part of the constitutions of eleven states throughout the United States. Georgia was one of the states that passed such an amendment.

Leading up to the 2004 election and ballot measures, community activists in Georgia began organizing grassroots campaigns to fight the constitutional amendments. They facilitated a series of town meetings to design the campaign against the proposed amendment and mobilize the community. During these meetings, the importance of working with faith leaders was highlighted in great detail. Most of the harmful rhetoric was championed by individuals who claimed to speak for "God" and as "the voice of the religious community." The GLBT community and its allies needed to show that there was a different voice from communities of faith—one that spoke in support of equality and justice for the GLBT community and insisted on a shared humanity. Reverend Michael Robinson, along with other faith leaders, attended several of these meetings.

As a Baptist minister, Michael Robinson was not one to shy away from conversations about morality and values. Trained in a conservative, exclusively white Southern Baptist seminary, Michael was taught to believe that gay and lesbian relationships were wrong. While at school, he met a young theologian named Allen whom he respected deeply. After the two became friends, Allen came out to Michael as a gay man. Michael's experience of Allen as a friend and colleague provided a contrast with the negative stereotypes and prejudices he held regarding gay people, and the contradiction led Michael to reconsider the true meaning of his faith and his future work as a minister. He made a commitment to living out his spiritual beliefs as an ally of the GLBT community. Now a minister in an American Baptist congregation in Rome, Georgia, Michael openly challenged his church and community not just to think about their values and beliefs but to put those beliefs into practice.

The church that Michael served had a history of steadfast engagement in the civil rights struggles of African Americans in the 1960s and 1970s. When Michael came to the church in 1984, his deep commitment to social justice called him to lead his congregation in taking a public stand in support of the lesbian, gay, bisexual, and transgender community. After several years of reflection and dialogue, this small Southern Baptist church pledged to support the human dignity of all people, regardless of sexual orientation or gender identity, and to accept GLBT people as full members of the congregation. Now, with the constitutional amendment battle under way, Michael and his congregation had an opportunity not only to affirm GLBT individuals as members of their church community but to take a public stand in the larger community.

As an outgrowth of the needs identified during the community-wide meetings, a small group of individuals, including Michael, set out to organize religious leaders and communities of faith. This initially seemed like a daunting task. Bringing together leaders from diverse faith traditions in the South was sure to be challenging, especially since the topic of discussion was religion and GLBT rights. Some of the faith leaders they initially contacted expressed anger, disbelief, and condemnation. Yet, as the word spread about the work of the group, the group found widespread interest.

By making connections with colleagues in their communities and using existing networks within their own faith traditions, the small planning group grew to be a statewide coalition of more than three hundred religious leaders who were committed to speaking out publicly in support of the GLBT community and in opposition to the amendments. The coalition, called Voices of Faith for Change, found that many religious leaders felt as Michael did: they wanted to speak out in support of the GLBT community but were not sure how to do it. The organizing and networking done by the coalition gave religious leaders the opportunity to connect with one another and engage in this important work.

The religious leaders in this newly formed coalition knew that they held a powerful voice in the campaign against the Georgia constitutional amendment that promised sweeping discrimination against same-sex couples. Uncertain of how to proceed, coalition leaders contacted the GLBT activists who had led the community meetings. Together they planned a statewide rally and lobby day opposing the proposed state amendment. The rally would be called "Protecting All of Our Families: Defending Our Constitution," and it would focus on how citizens' faith called them to challenge the amendment. Voices of Faith for Change helped to mobilize more than two hundred people from every region of the state for the first statewide event led by religious leaders and people of faith in support of GLBT rights.

As part of the leadership team for the coalition, Michael had a significant role on the day of the lobby. He stood on the stage with leaders of multiple faith communities—Jewish, Buddhist, Unitarian, Christian, and Pagan—and challenged Georgia legislators to consider the historical ramifications of the proposed amendment. A burly man in a dark suit, Michael stood in the Georgia heat and asked the crowd of two hundred ministers, rabbis, and people of faith from around the state to think about the consequences of the impending legislation for their children and their congregations. "Will generations after us shudder at our ignorance and bigotry for denying people the right to marry because they happen to be attracted to people of the same sex?" he asked. "Will they wonder what kind of world could allow heterosexuals the right to marry no matter what crime they commit, or how many times they fail at it, but denies gays and lesbians the same human right no matter how long they have been together?" Michael also challenged his colleagues and those who question the morality of GLBT people with the following words: "The immorality does not rest with those who wish to express their love and commitment in same-sex marriage. The immorality rest with those of us who would deny people these basic human rights."

After the rally, clergy and lay leaders met with their legislative representatives to voice their opposition to the amendment by suggesting that a constitutional amendment would establish one religion's definition of marriage over the definitions of faith communities that embrace same-sex marriage. Many politicians had never before heard from religious leaders and people of faith who were supportive of GLBT rights. Members of the coalition were energized as they experienced how important their voices were in creating change.

They took a very public stand at the state capitol and created enormous momentum among the rally participants. They hoped that the groups would be able to carry this passion and commitment back to their local congregations and communities.

CORRESPONDING TEXTBOOK CHAPTERS

Chapter 17: Religion and spirituality, by D. F. Morrow & B. Tyson.
Chapter 19: Social welfare policy and advocacy, by L. Messinger.

ADDITIONAL READINGS

Ellison, M. (2004). *Same sex marriage? A Christian ethical analysis*. Cleveland, OH: Pilgrim Press.
People of Faith for Gay Civil Rights. (2005). *People of faith clearinghouse*. Retrieved June 7, 2005, from http://www.pfgcr.org.
Wolfson, E. (2004). *Why marriage matters: America, equality, and gay people's right to marry*. New York: Simon and Schuster.

QUESTIONS FOR DISCUSSION

1. What strengths do faith communities bring to organizing for GLBT social justice issues? What challenges or weaknesses might these communities face?

2. What specific issues might faith communities have as they become allies to GLBT people? How might they work through these issues?

3. How might racial, ethnic, or cultural dynamics affect GLBT organizing efforts in faith communities?

4. How would you suggest the leadership team of the religious coalition support local faith communities in sustaining their individual efforts as advocates?

5. Beyond organizing for a specific issue (i.e., opposing a state amendment), how might the religious coalition maintain its presence in advocating for GLBT rights?

EXERCISE

Name: Affirming Faith Communities in Action

Purpose: To identify GLBT affirming faith communities and their work at the national, state, and local levels for GLBT rights

Structure: Student groups will be assigned denominations or faith traditions to investigate, examining the gay-friendliness and pro-GLBT movements within each, and will report on them in the next class.

Implementation: The class will brainstorm religious and faith communities. Do they know the practices and policies of these faith traditions regarding GLBT members and working for GLBT rights? If the tradition as a whole is not fully supportive of GLBT members, what subsets exist within these communities that are affirming and supportive of full inclusion of GLBT people? Encourage students to think beyond the traditional Judeo-Christian faiths and include any of the major world religions or other spiritual and humanistic traditions. The class will be divided into five groups. Each group will identify one faith tradition or denomination and explore its policies and practices regarding GLBT members and working for GLBT rights. The instructor will note the tradition or denomination of each group to make sure that the groups do not overlap. Groups will research a chosen tradition (or subset) and address the following questions:

1. What are the policies regarding GLBT people as members of this faith community? Can GLBT individuals be full members? Can they be ordained as clergy or leaders in this tradition? If GLBT people are not able to be full members or be ordained leaders, what's the rationale for this policy?

2. What is the history of this faith community in accepting GLBT members and working on GLBT rights?

3. Does this faith community bless weddings/unions of same-sex couples?

4. What work has this community done on a national, statewide, or local level to affirm and/or advocate for GLBT people?

The instructor may also encourage students to attend a worship service or to interview a local member of each faith community. Students will prepare a 10–15 minute summary on their chosen faith community and present it during the following class period.

Suggested Social Work Courses: Community practice; spirituality and social work; social work policy

Suggested Class Size: 20–30 students

Materials and Time: No additional materials are needed. This activity could follow the case study discussion but would therefore be carried into the following class session. Student presentations and related discussion will last 45–75 minutes, depending on class size.

PART 5

POLICY AND RESEARCH

THE FINAL three chapters offer three different views of social workers: chapter 27 features a social work student, chapter 28 highlights the experiences and thoughts of a lobbyist in a statewide aging advocacy organization, and chapter 29 is told from the perspective of two social workers within an urban GLBT community center. Each of these social workers has a unique perspective rooted in their professional experiences and roles. Teachers in HBSE and practice courses could use these cases to challenge students to think about who they will be as practitioners: how their race, gender, class, religious affiliation, sexual orientation, geographical setting, and professional experience will inform their practice. The diversity of these characters also should enable all students to identify with one or another of the social workers in the cases, which will assist them in seeing the relevance of policy and research to their future practice.

27

HATE CRIME LAWS: MAKING A DIFFERENCE

Lori Messinger

JARED LIEBOWITZ could not believe that he was getting ready to testify before a meeting of Georgia's House Committee on Justice. He was supposed to explain the need for a new hate crime law that would add crimes based on sexual orientation, disability, and age to the current law, which was limited to crimes based on race, ethnicity, or religion. Jared was a 21-year-old white Jewish heterosexual, a male social work student from a suburban area of a state in the North—a fairly unlikely advocate for gay and lesbian issues in Georgia, even in his own mind. But a class project had led him to this new role.

Jared had been taking a required social work class on policy development and advocacy. To complete the class project, students worked together in small groups to identify a current bill and follow it through the state legislature. The bill had to have a social work or social welfare focus, and the group had to learn about the bill, analyze the bill using social work values and ethics, and take a position to support or oppose the bill on those grounds.

Jared's group had five members, and, as usual, he was the only man. One member of the group, Toni, identified openly as a lesbian, but the other four were straight. When they had looked through the bills pending in the legislature, they were very excited when they came upon the hate crime bill. Jared remembered Toni saying, "This would really make a difference, and not just for queer crime victims. It would just give queer people a sense that they are a group that experiences a unique kind of discrimination, different from racism or sexism but just as important." Jennifer, another of the group members, liked the idea of protecting people with disabilities, because she had a sister who had Down's syndrome. Jared just liked the general idea of fairness and justice that the bill entailed, so he supported the choice. With the final two members, Heather and Emily, not caring much one way or the other, the group decided that this would be their bill.

When the group divided up tasks, Jared offered to contact the gay and lesbian advocacy groups working to pass the bill, while Jennifer agreed to call someone she knew in the area of disability services to find out who was working on the bill from that perspective. Toni and Heather agreed to e-mail the legislators who were sponsoring the bill, and Emily would see what had been written on the Internet and in the papers about hate crime legislation in the state.

While each member of the group worked on his or her own area, Jared pretty quickly moved into a leadership role: setting meeting times, identifying tasks that needed to be done, following up with group members to make sure they were accomplishing their tasks, and identifying missing pieces in their final project. He also became the most invested in the bill, even more than Toni and Jennifer, who were too busy with their other classes and work to have much time to contribute to the project.

Jared met several times with leaders from Equality Now, a statewide advocacy organization for lesbian and gay issues, who gave the student group a treasure trove of information about the history of the bill, its sponsors, its opponents, and their plan for advocacy on the bill. They seemed to be the lead agency working to pass the bill.

Last Monday, Jared spoke at length with Thomas, the 28-year-old black gay man who worked as the legislative advocate with Equality Now. Jared was trying to understand why people opposed the inclusion of sexual orientation in the hate crime bill. He just didn't get why it would be such a problem; he had known gay and lesbian people all his life and had had queer friends in high school and college. He had seen gay men bullied in the locker room and the hallways in high school, and it always made him mad. It was so clearly wrong, he argued. Why not pass a law to make it a more serious crime to hurt someone out of hate?

Thomas said that he was glad that Jared felt that way, because it was important to have support from heterosexual allies for any legislation that helped gay and lesbian people. But opponents were raising other issues. Some who were fighting the bill argued that if this law were passed, people who did not approve of homosexuality could get in trouble for speaking out against it, that it would be seen as "hate speech." Thomas said that this was not even a possibility, given the constraints of the bill, which applied only to violent crimes. But other opponents had a more serious argument: that any addition of sexual orientation to the state law went a step closer to legally recognizing lesbians and gay men as members of an oppressed population. Jared noted that this was exactly the reason Toni liked the bill—because it recognized "queer people," as she said, as a group in need of protection. Thomas explained that if lesbian and gay people were seen as members of an identifiable discriminated population, they could better fight for their rights on other issues, like protections in housing, employment, and benefits like health insurance.

Jared thought about this for a long while and then noted, "But the law doesn't name lesbians and gay men. It says that no one, heterosexual or homosexual, can be assaulted on the basis of their sexual orientation. So it protects all people, people of any sexual orientation, all of us!" Thomas agreed, noting that all of the categories were phrased in a similar manner. "Perhaps you should speak on the legislation at the upcoming hearing," Thomas suggested, smiling at Jared. "It would be wonderful to have a straight ally speak out on this issue."

Jared was surprised by the invitation. "But I am just a student! No one wants to hear what I have to say."

"That's not true. You vote in this state, right?" asked Thomas.

"Sure."

"And you are educated about the issues, and the history of the bill, and the ways it impacts different groups. You would be the perfect person to speak to the bill. Can you make the hearing on Thursday of next week?" Thomas flipped through a worn calendar on his desk. "The hearing starts at ten a.m., but we probably won't get to speak until ten thirty or so. I will speak, and so will Debbie from the Disabilities Coalition and Jerry from AARP. You would speak after them. You probably won't have more than five minutes to make your point and get offstage."

"Well, I guess I could. I don't have class then." Jared could feel himself getting nervous. They had watched videotapes of people giving testimony and speaking in committee meetings, but it was hard to imagine doing it himself. "If I write a draft of what I would say, would you look it over?"

"Sure," Thomas agreed, smiling broadly. "Welcome to the fight! You are now officially an ally!"

That had been a week ago last Monday. Now here he was, stepping forward to speak out for equality. All at once, he felt like a real social worker.

CORRESPONDING TEXTBOOK CHAPTERS

Chapter 16: Violence, hate crimes, and hate language, by M. E. Swigonski.
Chapter 19: Social welfare policy and advocacy, by L. Messinger.

ADDITIONAL READINGS

Cahill, S., Ellen, M., & Tobias, S. (2002). *Family policy: Issues affecting gay, lesbian, bisexual, and transgendered families.* New York: National Gay and Lesbian Task Force Policy Institute.

Human Rights Campaign. (2003). *Statewide hate crimes laws.* Retrieved September 6, 2003, from http://www.hrc.org/state-action/hatecrime.pdf.

National Association of Social Workers. (2003). *Social work speaks* (6th ed.). Washington, DC: NASW Press.

National Gay and Lesbian Task Force. (2003). *The Local Law Enforcement Act: The appropriate next step in federal hate crimes law.* Retrieved July 12, 2003, from http://www.thetaskforce.org/downloads/fedhatecrimeslaw.pdf.

National Gay and Lesbian Task Force. (2003). *The Local Law Enforcement Enhancement Act: An important step in combating hate violence.* Retrieved July 12, 2003, from http://www.thetaskforce.org/downloads/locallawenfact.pdf.

QUESTIONS FOR DISCUSSION

1. Why would it be important to have a law in place that punishes violent crimes targeting lesbians and gay men? People with disabilities? Older people?

2. Can you identify any additional reasons someone might have for opposing this legislation?

3. Can you think of any unintended consequences of such a law?

4. What kinds of information would help Jared to prepare for his testimony? Where would you find this information?

5. What is the benefit of having someone who is not a member of an affected group testify on behalf of a bill? What are the limitations?

6. If you were in Jared's position, what personal, social, religious, or professional issues might affect your speaking out on behalf of GLBT people? Would it make a difference if you knew there would be press coverage of the committee meeting? Why or why not?

EXERCISE

Name: Policy Search for Allies

Purpose: To challenge students to identify policies that would improve the lives of lesbian and gay people; to give them practice in policy-related research; to give them practice in preparing public testimony

Structure: Two weeks before the in-class exercise, the class is divided into groups of five. Each group is assigned to research the bills currently (or recently) proposed in their own state legislature that relate to gay, lesbian, bisexual, and/or transgender (GLBT) state residents. While some bills are obviously related, like the one in the case study, others may be difficult to identify, because the implications for GLBT people and their families may not be openly discussed in the proposed legislation. Statewide and national GLBT advocacy organizations can be helpful in identifying these bills.

After each group selects a bill, they will contact the teacher and convey their choice, so the instructor can be sure that there is no duplication. Students will then determine the bill's stakeholders, the main arguments of supporters and opponents, the appropriate legislative committee in which the bill will be discussed, and the "social work stance" on the bill. Each group will prepare a 5-minute statement in support of their position on the bill in question. These statements will include their arguments and the way their role as social workers influences their decision to act regarding this bill. Finally, each group will select one student to introduce their bill, one to introduce the speechmaker, and a third to give the speech.

Implementation: A podium will be set up in the front of the classroom. The teacher will play the role of the committee chair, introducing hearings on each of the different bills. The instructor will need the numbers and names of the bills and will call for each in numerical order. When a group's bill is called, one student will read the name of the bill and explain its purpose. A second student will introduce the speechmaker; students could be encouraged to embellish here by pretending that the speechmaker represents a specific social agency or has certain expertise that should be included in the introduction. Speakers will be given 5 minutes for their statements, with the teacher giving them a 1-minute warning before their time expires. After each statement is completed, the rest of the class will encouraged to ask three or four clarifying questions of the presenting group. At the end of the short question-and-answer period, the teacher will cut off conversation and move the discussion on to the next bill. This process will be repeated until all groups have completed their presentations.

After all of the presentations, the teacher will lead the whole class in a debriefing session. Questions might include:

1. What was it like to speak in this kind of structured setting?
2. Did it make it seem more possible that you might speak out on a bill in a real committee hearing?
3. What was the most difficult part of preparing for the speech? Was it finding information, determining the "social work stance," being an advocate on a GLBT issue, or something else?
4. Were you persuaded by your colleagues' presentations? Do you think legislators would be persuaded? If not, why not?
5. Besides testimony, what could you do to advocate for your bill?
6. What chance do you think your bill has in the upcoming session?

Suggested Social Work Courses: Social welfare policy; practice with GLBT populations
Suggested Class Size: 20–25 students
Materials and Time: A podium would be helpful, but no other materials are needed. Students will need at least two weeks to prepare for in-class presentations. The presentations and related discussion will probably last 45–75 minutes, depending on the number of groups.

28

A POLICY ANALYSIS OF A CONSTITUTIONAL DOMA AMENDMENT: IMPLICATIONS FOR AGING POPULATIONS

Lori Messinger

WHEN ELVIRA ORTEGA, MSW, reached her office at the State Coalition for Successful Aging on Monday morning, she found more than twenty-five e-mails waiting for her. She smiled, thinking that the number would quadruple when the legislative session opened in two months. As she quickly browsed through them she came upon one, from another lobbyist, with the heading "Need Your Help to Oppose the Gay Marriage Amendment." Her gut reaction was to delete it; Elvira couldn't imagine why her group would enter into that mess. It was a lose-lose issue—sure to alienate traditional supporters if the group opposed the amendment and sure to alienate lesbian and gay supporters if they supported it. There had been a number of polls about the issue, and it seemed certain to win in the upcoming legislative session and popular vote. While she didn't personally support the amendment, seeing it as unnecessary, she could use her job only to support causes that related to the mission of the organization. But she was curious: why would the other lobbyist see this amendment as an issue facing the elderly? ·

She opened the e-mail and read:

Dear Elvira:

I know you may be surprised to see this message from me. I have been hired to work with the statewide gay rights coalition to fight the Gay Marriage Amendment in the upcoming legislative session. While you may not see the connection between this legislation and your constituency, I assure you that there is one.

The second section of the amendment is the one that affects your folks. It states that "no legal status for unmarried persons shall be created or recognized by this state or its political subdivisions that is similar to that of marriage." That could be interpreted to include contracts between heterosexual people living together. I looked it up and found that more than 29% of elderly persons in our state whose partners have died are living with (and not married to) new partners. The rights of these unmarried partners to pass on material goods and make medical and funereal decisions are essentially voided by this amendment, which would give family members precedence over the unmarried partner, even if the partner is named in a will, power of attorney, or other legal document.

We would really like the official and organizational support of your agency in this fight. Do a little digging and see what your organization wants to do. I am free to meet anytime in the next week.

Best,
Thomas Park
Lobbyist, Citizens for Fairness

Elvira pulled her copy of the state's *Report on Aging* from her bookshelf and flipped through the charts on residential patterns. Thomas was right, of course. Not only did 29% of widows and widowers live with an unmarried partner, but 15% of unmarried or widowed women lived with a female friend. Elvira knew from her practice experiences that these women often expected one other to oversee their medical care in the event of a health crisis. And that was not counting those who were actually in same-sex intimate relationships—no one had any good numbers on that. If medical powers of attorney would not be upheld in courts, as a result of this amendment, there would be serious consequences for elders in the state.

Elvira tried to imagine taking this issue to the organization's executive director and the board of directors. She knew their concerns: taking a stand in opposition to the amendment would offend the organization's elderly supporters who were religious conservatives, and their donations would decrease as a result. Also, legislators whose support they needed on other aging policies might withdraw that support if they viewed the organization as opposing the amendment. Finally, there would surely be some opposition from the board of directors, who would see this as more of a gay issue and one that was inappropriate for an aging-advocacy organization. Basically, she thought, it just wasn't smart. There was no real political upside to joining the anti-amendment coalition.

Yet she found herself struggling with the idea anyway. She remembered the NASW *Code of Ethics* and its requirement to fight discrimination against any group. Lesbian and gay elderly, and unmarried elderly couples, and friends living together in mutual care situations would all be adversely affected by the amendment—and these were her constituents.

Perhaps she could propose that the State Coalition for Successful Aging offer to send out literature about the amendment to its mailing list but not formally take a position on the amendment itself. That would certainly expand the reach of the anti-amendment forces, but it would not cost the agency politically. Not really satisfied with the idea, but committed to providing some kind of support, Elvira walked down to the executive director's office to discuss the amendment and its implications for elderly people in the state.

CORRESPONDING TEXTBOOK CHAPTERS

Chapter 13: Gay, lesbian, bisexual, and transgender older people, by E. M. Fullmer
Chapter 19: Social welfare policy and advocacy, by L. Messinger

ADDITIONAL READINGS

Cahill, S., South, K., & Spade, J. (2000). *Outing age: Public policy issues affecting gay, lesbian, bisexual, and transgender elders.* New York: National Gay and Lesbian Task Force.
Grossman, A., D'Augelli, A., & O'Connell, T. (2001). Being lesbian, gay, bisexual, and 60 or older in North America. *Journal of Gay and Lesbian Social Services, 13*(4), 23–40.
Mizrahi, T. (2001). Basic principles for organizing: Perspectives from practice. In A. R. Roberts & G. Greene (Eds.), *The social work desk reference* (pp. 517–524). New York: Oxford University Press.
Nystrom, N. M., & Jones, T. C. (2003). Community building with aging and old lesbians. *American Journal of Community Psychology, 31*(3–4), 293–300.

QUESTIONS FOR DISCUSSION

1. What is the social work position regarding the gay marriage amendment?
2. Who is protected or helped if this amendment passes?
3. With what other groups could the Citizens for Fairness coalition work? Would some be easier than others?
4. What other policy issues affecting the elderly also have a specific impact on GLBT people?

EXERCISE

Name: Analyzing GLBT policies with respect to their implications for others
Purpose: Students will learn to consider the many implications of GLBT-related policies for GLBT and heterosexual persons. Students will use critical-thinking skills to understand the different constituencies that might form coalitions to fight discriminatory policies and support GLBT-friendly legislation.

Structure: Students will work in small groups to analyze a proposed GLBT-related policy initiative. They will then consider how these analyses inform coalition building in policy advocacy.

Implementation: The instructor will select a recently proposed or current policy directed at GLBT people or issues in your state. (Examples include bills disallowing GLBT people from being adoptive or foster parents, hate crime bills targeting crimes based on sexual orientation, constitutional amendments disallowing gay marriage, and employment protections for GLBT people. Instructors can find relevant bills on the Human Rights Campaign Web site, under legislation by state.) As a class, students will consider the implications of this policy for GLBT people in your state. Students will identify other groups in your state that might be affected by the bill. Examples include children, human services professionals, educators, law enforcement personnel, heterosexual unmarried couples, elderly people, and small-business owners. Students will divide into groups, each one representing an interested party that they identified. Each group should answer the following questions:

1. How would the proposed policy affect your group if it were implemented?
2. What kind of advocacy organizations related to your group would be interested in this bill? Would they support or oppose the bill?
3. Could the bill be amended to address your group's concerns? If so, would the organization change its position on the bill?
4. How would the advocacy organization stimulate interest about the bill with its constituency?
5. Would the advocacy organization be likely to join a coalition supporting/opposing this bill? Would individual members of your group? Why or why not?
6. What is the stance of the *NASW Code of Ethics* on this bill?

Students will come back together and present their answers to the group.

Suggested Social Work Courses: Social welfare policy; social work with aging populations

Suggested Class Size: Any size class would be suitable.

Materials and Time: The initial discussion will take 20 minutes. The group work will require 20–30 minutes, and the in-class reporting and discussion will need 20–30 minutes.

29

GETTING IT RIGHT: DOING RESEARCH WITH GLBT YOUTHS

Lori Messinger

HOPE SAMUELS, BSW, was very excited when she saw the new "Request for Proposals" from the Youth Leadership Foundation. The organization was offering a grant for leadership development with youths of color, rural youths, or GLBT (gay, lesbian, bisexual, and transgender) youths. Hope had wanted to create a program like that since she started working as the youth coordinator at the Omaha GLBT Community Center two years ago. She ran social groups and coming out groups for GLBT youths who were 12–19 years old, but there was nothing to help these young people learn to advocate for themselves and make a difference in the community. She had good ideas about how to design the program, partner agencies they could work with in the larger community, and other potential funding sources who could help them meet the grant's requirement for matching funds. Yet when she read the instructions for the grant proposal and saw that the foundation required that all grant recipients evaluate the success of their new program, she started to worry.

The four-person staff at the community center ran a number of programs: a sexual health education service, a buddy program for people living with AIDS, youth and adult support groups, and a community education program, as well as programming workshops and events for local GLBT residents. While they kept records of the numbers of people served, the center staff had no formal evaluation process. But the foundation seemed to want more information than mere attendance; they wanted each grant recipient to identify program goals and objectives and then to measure how well those objectives were accomplished. Hope wasn't sure how to approach this new task, so she went to talk to Kishawn Sims, MSW, the community center's executive director.

"Kishawn," Hope said, handing her a copy of the "Request for Proposals," "this grant looks like a great opportunity for us, but they require an evaluation. I can come up with a list of goals and objectives for a leadership development program, but I'm not sure what to do to evaluate it. Any ideas?"

Kishawn skimmed the grant instructions, focusing on the evaluation section. "Well, tell me about your goals and objectives, and we can work from there."

"Well, I think the big goals would be to improve the youths' sense of self, to teach them advocacy skills, and to assist them in implementing projects to improve the GLBT community," Hope replied, ticking the goals off on her fingers.

Kishawn wrote the goals on the left side of a piece of paper and looked back at Hope. "Okay, so let's come up with our objectives," she said.

They worked on the objectives for another fifteen minutes and came up with the following:

GOALS	OBJECTIVES
1. improve the youths' sense of self	a. improve youths' self-esteem b. improve youths' comfort with their sexual orientation c. help youths see themselves as capable of creating changes in their communities
2. teach youths advocacy skills	a. provide 8–10 youths (ages 12–19) with training about advocacy b. improve youths' knowledge about advocacy
3. assist youths in implementing projects to improve local GLBT communities	a. lead youth work in small groups to design and implement successful community projects b. teach evaluation measures to youths

"Okay," said Kishawn, "now we have to think about how we would assess our performance on each of the objectives."

"Well, Objective 2a could be met by counting the number of youths attending training," said Hope. "And I guess we could do the same thing to record the youths creating projects and our teaching them evaluation methods."

"Yeah, but then it gets a little harder," replied Kishawn. "For the other objectives, we need to think about other ways to get feedback on how we're doing, feedback directly from the youths."

"Well, if we want to know what they think about themselves, for Objectives 1a, 1b, 1c, and 2b, we could ask them to fill out some sort of survey," said Hope. "We could have them rate themselves on self-esteem, comfort with their sexual orientation, sense of themselves as capable of facilitating change, and knowledge of advocacy skills at the beginning of the program and then again at the end, to see if it made any difference."

"I'm not sure that we can get them to fill out any surveys, especially ones about their feelings, without asking their parents' permission," Kishawn replied.

"What if they were anonymous? Would it still be a problem?" Hope asked.

"Well, I think it is really about them being minors. I don't think you can do research with minors without a parent's permission," Kishawn responded.

"That would be a problem," Hope said. "Lots of the kids in the support group and the coming out group don't tell their parents that they are coming here. They might decide not to participate if they had to get some sort of permission slip signed.

"The grant proposal also wants us to identify the age, race, ethnicity, and gender of our participants," she noted, pointing to the instructions. "Couldn't that kind of information be a problem with confidentiality? I mean, we only have one Indian in the group, and only three black kids. If we kept that information, wouldn't outside people be able to figure out who these kids are?"

"Yeah. And how do we get Gina to identify her gender? Do we go by her biological gender or her preferred gender?" asked Kishawn.

"This could get a little tricky," Hope agreed.

"Well, let me check with a professor friend of mine at the school of social work," said Kishawn. "She'll know what the rules are about research with kids, and she might have some other ideas about these other issues. In the meantime, why don't you work on the grant proposal and I'll work on developing the evaluation section?"

"That sounds great," Hope agreed, gathering up the grant materials. "The deadline is the end of the month, so we have a little over two weeks. I'll try to get my part to you in a week"

"Great. I'll let you know what I hear."

Hope went back to her desk, excited and hopeful about the prospect of creating the new youth leadership program.

CORRESPONDING TEXTBOOK CHAPTERS

Chapter 8: Gay, lesbian, bisexual, and transgender adolescents, by D. F. Morrow.
Chapter 20: Toward affirmative practice, by L. Messinger.

ADDITIONAL READINGS

Herek, G. M., Gillis, J. R., Cogan, J. C., & Glunt, E. K. (1991). Avoiding heterosexist bias in psychological research. *American Psychologist, 44*(9), 957–963.

Martin, J. I., & Knox, J. (2000). Methodological and ethical issues in research on lesbians and gay men. *Social Work, 24*(1), 51–59.

QUESTIONS FOR DISCUSSION

1. What specific issues do GLBT youth face in their communities?

2. What are the potential benefits of a leadership development program for these youths?

3. What are the needs of FLBT teens regarding confidentiality and self-determination? How would you ethically meet their needs while acknowledging their vulnerability and the rights of their parents?

4. What barriers might a new leadership development program face (e.g., youth participation, community support, parental approval, etc.)?

5. If you were Hope Samuels, what are the next steps you would take to develop the youth leadership program?

6. Besides meeting the requirements of the funder, what are the benefits of creating a process to evaluate the leadership program? What are the complications?

EXERCISE

Name: Developing a Client Survey

Purpose: To hone students' sensitivity to the ways in which gender and sexual orientation affect the development of research instruments; to develop skills in designing surveys that are appropriate for use with GLBT populations

Structure: Students will be asked to design a survey for use with youths participating in the leadership development program described in the case study.

Implementation: Before the class meeting, students will read the case study. In class, students will be divided into groups of four or five. Each group will develop a survey that would help assess the goals and objectives delineated in the case study, as well as considering methods for administering the survey and ways to address the many confidentiality and data collection concerns raised by Hope and Kishawn in the case study. Students will have 20–30 minutes to design their survey. When they are finished, each group will present its survey and its plan for administration.

Suggested Social Work Courses: Social work research

Suggested Class Size: Any size class would be suitable.

Materials and Time: 20–30 minutes for the group work and 20–30 minutes for in-class discussion of the groups' surveys and plans

All three women are in the mess hall at lunch, several days after Janice and Lynn were at the lesbian bar. Janice is seated at a lunch table. She and Caroline have just finished a brief work-related conversation, and Caroline is walking away to sit at a table nearby. Lynn comes up and wants to sit with Janice and connect to her as a lesbian. Caroline *probably* will not be able to hear their conversation.

JANICE: The setting is an air force base located in a small Southern town. You are an African American lesbian, and your career is the military. On base you put on a tough front as a military police office (MP). Because of your job position, you are out to no one on base. For fear of being "outed," you rarely socialize with anyone on base, either heterosexual or gay. Isolation is killing you, so you search the Internet and find a gay bar in a nearby city. In civilian clothes, you go there and talk with several lesbians. Leaving the bar with a woman, you see Caroline drive by in her car.

CAROLINE: You are a heterosexual white female who is also an MP. Officially, you are a stickler for rules and protocol. Unofficially, you are one of the "good ol' boys" and think "dykes and fags" are perverted freaks of nature. They disgust you. You follow the rules at work, but you privately think those who are not white are inferior and should be put in their place. You have become rigid in your views of people. Being an MP feeds into your superiority over others. You have not seen Janice at the lesbian bar.

LYNN: You are a white lesbian on this same military base. You socialize with both male and female peers. You are out to three close friends on base, but you must still live under the "don't ask, don't tell" military policy. However, the unspoken truth among many is that you are a lesbian. You are also at the same bar that Janice goes to, but she does not see you. You recognize her as an MP on base, but she does not recognize you. You also know who Caroline is (her role and rank), but do not know much about her. You do not know that as she left the bar, Janice saw Caroline drive by.

LYNETTE. You are a 30-year-old white female who is hard of hearing. You wear hearing aids in both ears. You identify strongly as a lesbian and as a part of the deaf and hard-of-hearing community. You have been involved politically in gay rights groups and in deaf rights groups. You have been coming to group for eight months and consider yourself one of the "old-timers" in the group.

BARBARA. You are one of the facilitators of the group. You have been facilitating the group for a year and a half. You are 55 and white. You began having relationships with women after you divorced your husband. You have had feelings of same-sex attraction since your early teens, but you had felt those feelings were wrong and shameful. You married, had kids, and in your mid-forties after your kids had left home, you became quite unhappy and unfulfilled in life. You went through some counseling and determined that those feelings of same-sex attraction that you had stuffed away so long ago, were resurfacing. Eventually, you did divorce, and three years ago you met a woman with whom you fell in love—Theresa—and you've been with her ever since.

MARIA. You are one of the facilitators of the group. You began facilitating the group with Barbara a year and a half ago. You are 25 and Hispanic. You have been attracted to females since middle school. You tried dating boys a couple of times, but it didn't feel right. You are not in a committed relationship right now; you prefer to date different women rather than settling down with one particular woman. You feel confident about who you are; however, you haven't told your family that you are a lesbian because they are strict Catholics and you are convinced they would not accept your sexual orientation.

KEISHA. You are an African American college student who has been in the group for two months. You have always been attracted to men and have had several boyfriends since your early teens. Recently, you met a woman, Michelle, in a class, and you have become good friends with her. Michelle told you right away that she is gay and comfortable with who she is. You find yourself attracted to Michelle—but to Michelle only, no other females. So you aren't sure whether you are bisexual, gay, or heterosexual but just happen to be attracted to one particular woman.

LESLIE ANNE. You are a white 45-year-old female who has come to the group for the first time. You are shy and anxious about being in the group. You have recently come out of a fifteen-year relationship with another woman. Both of you are teachers, and both of you were very closeted during the time you were together.

BOBBI. You are a 30-year-old African American transgender woman. You were born a woman; however, you don't feel like you are a "traditional woman" or like a man. You consider yourself gender ambiguous, like your name, and you are comfortable with this. You often dress in men's clothes and don't correct people if they call you "sir." You are attracted to and date other women.